THE SHITTY COMMITTEE

YOUR GO-TO GUIDE ON HOW TO STOP FEELING LIKE SHIT AND START LIVING A MORE FULFILLING LIFE

JACK WILLIAMSON

THE SHITTY COMMITTEE

YOUR GO TO GUIDE ON HOW TO
STOP FEELING LIKE SHIT AND
START LIVING A MORE FULFILLING LIFE

JACK WILLIAMSON

M&Y PUBLISHING

DISCLAIMERS

Every effort has been made by the author and publishing house to ensure that the information contained in this book was correct as of press time. The author and publishing house hereby disclaim and do not assume liability for any injury, loss, damage, or disruption caused by errors or omissions, regardless of whether any error or omissions result from negligence, accident, or any other cause. Readers are encouraged to verify any information contained in this book prior to taking any action on the information.

The advice, tools and techniques shared in this book are there to help support and enhance your mental health, and not intended to replace professional help should it be required. If you require professional help around your own mental health please contact your GP, or if in crisis please contact the Samaritans on 116 123.

THE SHITTY COMMITTEE may be purchased for education, business, sales or promotional use. For information, please email enquiries@jackwilliamson.co.uk

Published by M&Y Publishing

First Edition

Edited by Lynne Best at The Fourth Pillar

Cover Design by Aaniyah Ahmed

ISBN 9798468242711

USEFUL DISCLAIMERS

If you suffer from ***Kakologophobia*** (aka a fear of curse words) this book is not for you.

If you are okay with swear words but have an issue with the C word, skip pages 68 to 72. Though I encourage you to be comfortable in your uncomfortableness with the word, as the exercises on those pages will really help you to master The Shitty Committee.

Though the stories within this book are all true, the names and some of the details of clients I mention in this book have been purposely altered to respect their confidentiality.

This is an interactive book, with space on the pages for you to write down your thoughts and answers to the questions asked. So keep a pen alongside you when reading this book and don't be afraid to go to town with your notes.

Alternatively, you can use your own notebook, or get a FREE copy of the accompanying workbook by scanning the QR code below.

DEDICATION

I would like to dedicate this book to my brother Alfie Williamson, who just shy of his 30th birthday lost the battle with his own Shitty Committee in 2015.

And to all of those who struggle day in and day out with The Shitty Committee, your strength to persevere through continues to inspire me.

CONTENTS

INTRODUCTION

On Monday 21st December 2015 at 8:03pm, my whole life was pulled from right underneath me.

I was having dinner with a dear friend of mine, Jin Jin, when my mum called unexpectedly. Unlike so many in the modern age who are attached to their phones and respond to any correspondence that comes in, I ignored the call, wanting to remain fully present with Jin Jin; but something niggled within me as my mum never calls me, she always messages, and so when I saw a voicemail pop up, I knew something was wrong.

Excusing myself to listen to the message, my mum's calm tone and demeanour on the phone as she said '*Hi Jack, this is mum, I need you to give me a call as soon as you get this*' immediately made me think something had happened to my brother. Call it intuition, a gut feeling, whatever you will, as I quickly dialled my mum back asking what was wrong, she said '*I need you to come home now*.' By that point I just knew '*It's Alfie isn't it, he's dead*' which my mum didn't acknowledge and just repeated the words '*I need you to come home now*.'

Understandably needing to cut the dinner short, Jin Jin kindly offered to drive me from Central London all the way to my mum's house on what felt like the longest drive of my life. As we turned into the road to see two police cars and an ambulance outside the house, my worst nightmare had been confirmed. Entering the house that I'd grown up in since the age of four, I walked straight past the living room where some of my relatives, including my estranged dad, had gathered and saw my mum in the kitchen, where she confirmed that my brother, Alfie, had taken his life.

At that moment, a mere second after starting to process what my mum had just said, she pleaded '*Promise you'll never do this to me.*' Having battled with depression throughout my entire life and having previously attempted to take my own life four times, including just nine months earlier, I wasn't in a space to be able to promise that I would never take my own life. But as the night wore on and the reality of what had happened began to sink in, it also dawned on me that if I was going to promise to anyone that I would never take my own life, I would need to make that promise and that commitment to myself.

Sadly, I will never know what was going through my brother's head that led him to take his own life but through processing my grief I have accepted and made peace with it. Whatever it was that led my brother to do so, I realised that *suicide is a permanent solution to a temporary problem*.

Sitting there that night trying to process what happened, away from all the other members of my extended family, I realised that my brain has an interesting way of processing traumatic events in my life. My initial reaction is to go into organisation mode and, given we were then just three days away from Christmas and the standstill it brings, I started planning out all the actions we would need to take around the funeral.

As I looked in my diary to plan these things, I noted the significance of the date in the calendar; for 21st December not only will forever be etched in my mind as the day my brother died, but it also marks the Winter Solstice in the Northern Hemisphere, the darkest day (in terms of daylight hours) in the calendar year. The symbolism was not lost on me that my brother took his life on the darkest day of the year. I made a note to myself that every day after that darkest of days, the world would get a little lighter in small ways that may be inconceivable at the time, but those small changes, like the extra minute or two of sunlight each day that follows up to the Summer Solstice, would make the world a little lighter, a little brighter.

That next day whilst helping to organise all of the funeral arrangements and arranging compassionate leave from work, I decided to also choose me. I decided to focus on looking after myself and start processing what had happened, especially as I was at high risk owing to also having a history with suicide. One expression kept playing over and over in my head and it's something I want you to keep in your mind as you go through this book...

YOUR TRAUMA ISN'T YOUR FAULT, BUT YOUR HEALING IS YOUR RESPONSIBILITY

So I embarked on intensive daily therapy sessions for the next month, gradually reducing down to weekly sessions by the end of the third month to help me understand and process the trauma I was going through, the grief I was experiencing, the thoughts I had and more. For if I didn't focus on processing the pain I was feeling, *the pain that was not transformed would be transmitted*, and if I didn't take responsibility for my own healing, it could impact and impede my relationships with friends, family, work colleagues and, most importantly, myself.

Over the next few years, I simultaneously continued to work in the music industry whilst also working on myself. I diversified my skill set by training and qualifying as a coach, psychotherapist, NLP practitioner, recovery specialist and more, so that I could make the transition out of working in marketing and international for record labels to supporting the mental health and well-being needs primarily of artists, actors and athletes, but also individuals from all different walks of life. I'm not going to lie to you - that road was often as bumpy as hell, as some of the stories in this book will tell, and 'The Shitty Committee' would often show up unannounced to make it even more hellish; but through my own life experience and the tools and techniques I've learnt along the way that I will share with you in this book, I was able to navigate my way through these bumps, diversions, setbacks and more to move forward to continue to live a more meaningful and fulfilling life.

It was on this journey, shortly after I decided to become sober on New Year's Day 2018 that I first heard the term The Shitty Committee whilst sitting with my friend Tinkerbell (no that's not her real name, but a name I have called her for the 20+ year's I've known her) in an AA meeting. We will cover exactly what it is in more detail in the next section, but in brief The Shitty Committee is something we all face in our lives. Whilst some people have mastered how to deal with it, many of us are often slaves to it, and I realised that my brother had become a slave to his own Shitty Committee, so much so that he couldn't see a way out of the control it had over him, which led him to take the action he did.

My life's purpose since 21st December 2015 has been to make sure that no one I know or work with goes through what I went through with my brother, for it was the worst day of my life. But I now also see it as the best day of my life; for that day I had a relation-shift to the relationship I have with myself, which has led me to understand The Shitty Committee more and, over time, no longer allow it to continue to make me feel like shit, and I want to do the same for you.

So, if you are ready to embark on this journey with yourself, let's get stuck in. It will at times be uncomfortable, but I want you to learn to become comfortable within your uncomfortableness. I promise you that what is on the other side of your uncomfortableness will be more than worth it.

SECTION 1

GETTING TO KNOW THE SHITTY COMMITTEE

1

WHAT IS THE SHITTY COMMITTEE?

"You have survived 100% of your darkest days, you will survive this too."
– Jack Williamson

In April 2019, a BBC journalist contacted me following the launch of a new initiative that I had partnered on with artist Lewis Capaldi and his manager, Ryan Walter, called LIVELIVE. The initiative provides emotional support to individuals attending concerts who may struggle with general anxiety, social anxiety, panic attacks or other mental health issues to make the concert-going experience more inclusive for all, and the journalist had called to ask if Lewis would be available to appear on BBC Breakfast to talk about the initiative.

At the time, Lewis had just scored a global Number 1 single with '*Someone You Loved*' and was gearing up for his debut album release. He was therefore unavailable to do the interview and in relaying this back to the journalist, she asked if I would be available to come on and talk about the LIVELIVE initiative instead. Questions and statements immediately started running through my head including '*Who are you to speak on this subject?*' '*No one's interested in what you have to say!*' and '*You're just a pity ask because who they want is unavailable!*' With the journalist's question still hanging in the air, I said I would let the journalist know after checking with Lewis's team and would come back to her later that day. To my surprise, however, she said they wanted to run with the piece the next morning (a mere 16 hours later) and would need an answer in the next hour.

With little to no time to think, I had to make a decision. This was an amazing opportunity for the LIVELIVE initiative - the first of its kind anywhere in the world - to get the attention it deserved on day-time television, but with me at the helm as opposed to the artist who was the face of the initiative. Whilst my team and I would be delivering the initiative at venues across the UK and Ireland, I didn't feel I could do the initiative justice - I was crippled with doubt. Within the next few minutes, Ryan had convinced me that it was a good idea and said that I would have both of their blessings to appear on BBC Breakfast. An hour later, I'd called the journalist back to confirm and was on a train from London to Manchester.

Even though the BBC Breakfast team had kindly shared the interview questions with me in advance, I was barely able to sleep that night. Thoughts raced around my head, like Lewis Hamilton on a Formula 1 circuit. '*You're going to fuck up live on national television,*' '*you're going to forget all the answers to the questions*', '*you're going to become a laughing-stock to anyone watching.*' On and on it went for the next couple of hours, until I managed to fall asleep for about 90 minutes before my alarm went off at 4:30am. Whenever my mind is in that space, I like to go to the gym to work off that energy and harness it into something good, but I was 300 miles away from home with no access to any facilities. So, I was left with myself and my thoughts replaying over and over again as I got ready for the interview.

Given that I'd worked in the music industry for over 18 years by that point and had been to countless TV shows all over the world with artists, prepping them for media appearances, you'd think I would be somewhat of a pro at getting myself hyped up for the interview - but you'd be wrong. I was there at the TV studio on my own, without anyone else but my own thoughts. As the time edged ever closer, I could feel the nerves continuing to build and, to avoid any further pressure, I turned my phone off so that I wouldn't be distracted by any messages from family or friends. I tried to focus on my breathing, whilst the voices of RuPaul saying '*And don't fuck it up*' and Bo Selecta's Davina McCall saying '*You are live on Big Brother, do not say fuck or bugger*' played over and over in my head like a record stuck on repeat. I wanted to run back to the hotel and escape this uncomfortable feeling I was experiencing, but before I knew it, I was ushered into the studio for my segment.

As I walked into the studio, I managed to quieten all the negative thoughts and asked myself '*What would you tell an artist if they were just about to be interviewed on TV?*' I told myself '*Just imagine you are popping over to BBC's Charlie and Naga's house for a coffee and a catch up and ignore everything and everyone else.*' As the videotape (VT) was rolling to introduce the segment, I sat down on the sofa to get ready for the interview. Naga kindly introduced herself and asked a couple of questions, likely sensing my nerves; we bonded over both living in and around Greenwich and, when the VT finished, we were live on air and before I knew it the interview was over.

The time went by in a flash and what was a 6-minute segment flew by in a matter of seconds. As I made my way back to the hotel, I felt an overwhelming sense of relief that I made it through the interview in one piece. Before reconnecting with others, I hit the gym to work through the adrenaline that was pumping through my body and grabbed breakfast and a Red Bull before making my way to the station to catch the train back to London. As I settled into the train journey, I eventually turned my phone back on, where I was met with a whole host of wonderful comments from friends who had got up early (7am on an Easter Saturday no less) to tune in and see my interview. Many had picked up on Charlie's comment about my soothing voice, which I thought had been said off air, and the majority had shared that I came across as calm, collected and articulate.

My mum, by now the only immediate member of my family left in my life, also shared words of encouragement about my interview. However, when speaking to my nan (my mum's mum), she was less than welcoming with her feedback, saying '*I could tell you were nervous, your mouth dried up a couple of times and you just looked uncomfortable sitting there.*' After all the wonderful words that had been shared with me by friends and my mum, it wasn't those that I focused on, but the negative remarks that my nan had said. Thankfully I didn't allow myself to stay in that mindset for too long; I was able to be with my friends, Kate and Tinkerbell, who responded to my Nan's observations by saying '*Wouldn't anyone be nervous and uncomfortable being on TV for the first time in their lives?*'

Why am I telling you this story and what does that have to do with you or The Shitty Committee? Well, this story gives some clear examples of not only what The Shitty Committee ***is*** but also what The Shitty Committee ***is not***. Have you ever found yourself in a situation where you are just about to do something, but you talk yourself out of it? Or how about where you think of a great idea, only to have others deconstruct that great idea to such a point where it no longer feels like a great idea but a bad one? Or how about when you've tucked into a takeaway to make you feel better only to feel worse afterwards?

If you are like me, then you will have likely experienced all three of those examples, and that is what The Shitty Committee is. It is the things in life that make you feel shit like shit and get in the way of you being able to live a truly fulfilling life. The Shitty Committee can be broken down into three main categories:

1. The Internal Shitty Committee
2. The External Shitty Committee
3. The Consumable Shitty Committee

Over the next three chapters in Section 1, we will take a look at each of the different categories that make up The Shitty

Committee, before moving on to Sections 2 and 3 on how to understand your own Shitty Committee, and how to master it to live a more fulfilling life.

So, let's begin with the first category; The Internal Shitty Committee.

2

THE INTERNAL SHITTY COMMITTEE

"Don't let your past steal your present."
– Cherrie L Moraga

The Internal Shitty Committee is formed of all those negative thoughts, beliefs, feelings or voices that run through your head on a daily, hourly or sometimes minute by minute basis, that band together and make you feel like shit.

I imagine that quite a few of you reading this will be thinking this is similar to what other people call *The Inner Critic*, *The Saboteur*, *The Shadow* (Carl Jung), *The Chimp Paradox* (Prof. Steve Peters) and many other titles, and to an extent you would be right. But I view The Internal Shitty Committee as more than those alternative titles, because I don't believe it is just one voice inside of us, but a collection of voices that have been gathered over time from our parents, relatives, society, the media, religion, friends, teachers, bullies, competitors and others to form a committee that makes us feel shitty, stepping up to the mic inside our heads dependent on the situation to share a negative thought, belief or feeling.

In the story I shared in Chapter 1 about my first appearance on TV, The Internal Shitty Committee consisted of a number of people stepping up to the mic inside my brain, including one of my old teachers '*who are you to speak on this subject?*', my nan '*no one's interested in what you have to say*', a bully who picked me last when playing sports '*you're just a pity ask because who they want isn't available*' and several others. Their views that I have carried with me from childhood to form limiting beliefs, were so strong when The Shitty Committee was sharing them, it was almost crippling and nearly prevented me from taking this opportunity, but through the support of Naga on the couch to ease my nerves and the support and blessing from Ryan and Lewis, I was able to overcome those negative voices inside to help me through.

The Internal Shitty Committee is connected to what is known in science terms as the reptilian brain, the part of our brain that goes back to our origins as a species, as cavepeople. Our reptilian brain was created with the primary purpose of keeping us safe from danger, back when we had to be aware of a tiger attack to being alert to poisonous berries. Whilst this purpose served us well, as our species evolved, our brains evolved as well, whereby today we have two other sections of the brain; the limbic section (the part of our brain that processes emotions and memory and reinforces our behaviour) and the neo-cortex section (the part of our brain that is responsible for our attention, thought, perception and episodic memory).

Unless you are someone like Joe Exotic or Carole Baskin who works with Tigers, we don't have to fear being attacked by one anymore, but our reptilian brain still finds it hard to distinguish from a real or perceived threat, which can help to explain why we can sometimes be so disturbed by nightmares we have as a child or even in adulthood. Depending on the thought, feeling or situation we find ourselves facing, the Internal Shitty Committee can be instantly triggered where it will pair up with the reptilian brain, pulling up to the mic anyone from The Internal Shitty Committee who can compound that feeling of danger with a message to keep you safe. But instead of keeping you safe, unless the perceived threat is real, the Internal Shitty Committee is keeping you stuck, making you its slave and preventing you from moving forward towards something you want or away from something you don't want.

Everything you want in life is just on the other side of fear itself and, as Nelson Mandela famously said, '*Our deepest fear is not that we are inadequate. Our deepest fear is that we are powerful beyond measure. It is our light, not our darkness that most frightens us. We ask ourselves who am I to be brilliant… As we are liberated from our own fear, our presence automatically liberates others.*'

The quote from Mandela makes it easy to identify the words used by The Shitty Committee to keep you where you are ('*who am I to be brilliant?*') The Internal Shitty Committee prays on your fear in order to keep you where you are, because there is safety in the familiar. The unknown is full of variables that The Internal Shitty Committee can't calculate for and that means it has to relinquish control of you, which it is unwilling to do. If you continue to allow it to retain control over your thoughts and feelings, it will ensure you remain its slave and prevent you from living a more fulfilling life.

In Section 2 of this book, we will look at your own Shitty Committee in more detail but, for now, having laid the foundations of what the Internal Shitty Committee is, we will move on to The External Shitty Committee.

3

THE EXTERNAL SHITTY COMMITTEE

"A tiger doesn't lose sleep over the opinions of a sheep."
- Proverb

Let's move on from The Internal Shitty Committee to The External Shitty Committee. The External Shitty Committee is about those negative people who *currently* surround you in your life, that make you feel worse about yourself.

A great example of this played out in a movie released in 2019 that helped to really highlight how The External Shitty Committee can have an adverse impact on your mental health. The movie in question revolved around lead character Arthur Fleck, a struggling clown and aspiring stand-up comedian, who lived with his poorly mother Penny in the early 1980s in Gotham City. Fleck, who suffered from a neurological disorder which impacted both his behaviour and his speech, had struggled to fit in since childhood and, when confronted with stressful situations, he would often display inappropriate responses.

Throughout the film, we see Fleck come under attack, verbally, physically or emotionally by nearly everyone he comes across. From the physical abuse at the hands of three delinquent businessmen on his commute home after losing his job or verbal abuse from fellow clowns with whom he interacts in his agency through to emotional abuse at the hands of his mum, we see the toll that this continued onslaught of what I call The External Shitty Committee was having on Fleck. At a stand-up show, Fleck's performance bombed; he was jeered and booed by the audience, further making him feel shit about himself. But when a clip of his performance went viral, he was invited on to a late-night show by the host who had made a mockery of Fleck's performance in the clip and sought revenge for the way the host and others made fun of him. This is where we see the birth of Joker, one of the most notorious villains of all time.

What this film helps to highlight is not only the impact that The External Shitty Committee can have on an individual, but how the constant barrage of verbal, physical or emotional abuse can stop someone from living a fulfilling life. It can lead them to breaking point where they snap or, as in the case of Arthur Fleck, seek revenge on those who had made a mockery of him.

In other shows, such as the critically acclaimed *13 Reasons Why* on Netflix, we see lead character Hannah Baker document via seven cassettes, 13 reasons why she ended up taking her own life. Each side of the cassette represented one individual from her school, who - whether they were aware of it or not - made her feel shit about herself to the point where she ended up taking her own life.

These two examples highlight the extreme ends of how The External Shitty Committee can impact how we feel about ourselves and give fuel to The Internal Shitty Committee, creating limiting beliefs about ourselves. In the Joker's case, the amalgamation of abuse from The External Shitty Committee was the straw that broke the camel's back, leading him into the criminal underworld; in Hannah Baker's case, The External Shitty Committee was like death by a thousand cuts, where she ended up taking permanent action to what had become too unbearable a situation to manage any longer.

However, The External Shitty Committee doesn't have to

produce extreme results like the examples above. In the story I shared in Chapter 1, my External Shitty Committee manifested itself in my Nan, who focused solely on criticising my appearance on TV and didn't offer any positive or neutral views; and whilst I know she means well, coming from a generation/background that focuses on the negative more than the positive, she doesn't necessarily realise how her words impact others. For others, it could be a partner who is always criticising your appearance, a boss who is always controlling what you do, a friend who always doubts your ability, a family member that always looks at things through a pessimistic lens, or a group that doesn't agree with the lifestyle you have chosen to live.

They are the individuals who can turn your positive news and experiences into a negative, magnify or enhance your insecurities rather than helping you to embrace or overcome them. They are the individuals who continually project their shitty thoughts, beliefs and views onto you, that can make you feel shit.

In many instances, those individuals are the people closest to you and they can often be threatened by your growth or want to hold you back from living a more fulfilling life; they may be envious of the pathway you are on and may throw obstacles in your way in the form of words (or physically) to keep you where you are in life. All of this behaviour by The External Shitty Committee gives massive fuel to The Internal Shitty Committee further holding you back from fulfilling your full potential.

In Section 2 of this book, we will delve into The External Shitty Committee, taking the time to identify who in your life forms your current External Shitty Committee and how they are serving you in your life. But before that, let's take a look at The Consumable Shitty Committee.

4

THE CONSUMABLE SHITTY COMMITTEE

"I'm just waiting to see if my coffee chooses to use its power for good or evil today." - Every Coffee Consumer

The Consumable Shitty Committee is the third and final type of Shitty Committee that can show up in our lives. It can be broken down into two main different areas – edible and non-edible consumption.

EDIBLE CONSUMPTION

When people first think of consumption, they think of food and drink. This actually forms part of The Consumable Shitty Committee, for what we put into our bodies can shape the way we feel about ourselves.

FOOD

I am the first to admit that I have a poor diet when it comes to food; my friends often joke about the food I eat being beige and, to be fair, they are right. Food has always been my biggest comfort when going through the motions with my emotions, but the junk food I consume as a quick fix that makes me feel good in the moment more often than not leaves me feeling both lethargic and worse about myself and the problems I'm facing. I'm sure many of you reading this have felt the same before.

Whilst in moderation most things are fine, including junk food, if you are continually consuming junk food or using it as a pick-me-up, it is more than likely to make you feel worse in the long run. Whether it be the lack of energy to be active (which gives fuel to The Internal Shitty Committee to call you lazy, unfit, unhealthy), changes to your physical appearance (which gives The Internal Shitty Committee the fuel to comment on what you wear, call you fat, ugly, or disgusting) or an impact on your physical health including immobility, damage to internal organs, rotting teeth, breakouts on the skin and more. The momentary high of junk food will be quickly replaced by the comedown afterwards.

CAFFEINE

Comedowns can be even worse when looking at the other types of edible consumption: caffeine, alcohol and drugs. Looking first at caffeinated drinks that are consumed, someone who regularly leans into coffee or energy drinks to get them through the day can experience extreme withdrawals if going cold turkey. This may result in migraines that will have those people reaching for painkillers or the caffeine once again to relieve the pain. However, we should be careful about our caffeine consumption, as caffeine is one of the six main contributors that can exacerbate anxiety (the other five being poor diet, alcohol, lack of sleep, stress and low energy). If consumed regularly in large quantities, it can increase the likelihood of a panic attack.

ALCOHOL AND DRUGS

Alcohol and drugs are the more common forms of The Consumable Shitty Committee that end up making people feel like shit. A significant number of people will consume alcohol or drugs to quieten or silence The Internal Shitty Committee, whether that be to make them feel more confident in a certain environment or to numb the pain of a trauma; but after the high comes the inevitable low. For aside from tequila (which is a stimulant), all other types of alcohol are depressants and can make us feel worse when drinking too much, bringing those emotions to the surface that we're trying to supress and making us feel like shit when the hangover kicks in. The same can occur with drugs too, whether they be prescription drugs or illegal drugs.

As mentioned with food, everything in moderation is okay and the purpose of this chapter is not to talk you out of eating junk food, drinking caffeine and alcohol, or taking drugs; the purpose of this chapter is to say that consuming too much of the wrong thing can lead to you feeling shit about yourself and take you further and further away from living a more fulfilling life.

We continue to see this played out time and again in the media with public figures who struggle with alcohol and drug addiction. We also see it in our own towns and cities where people are on the street and where consumption levels have impacted one's ability to live a 'normal' life, hold down a job, maintain a home, and preserve family life.

You don't have to lose everything to have The Consumable Shitty Committee make you feel shit about yourself and stop you from truly living a more fulfilling life. Up until my early thirties I was what people would call a thirsty bitch. Whilst I didn't drink frequently, when I did, I went all in on my drinking, and would often feel like shit the next day. Working in the music industry, my personal experience was that drinking and drug taking was encouraged; it allowed my drinking habits to blend in with others and let me rationalise my behaviour, because if others were doing it, it was okay for me to do it too. But, over time, it slowed down my ability to work, concentrate, be creative and pursue my dreams. So, for me, as a New Year's Resolution in 2018, I decided to quit drinking once and for all, and I have not looked back since.

For others, it may not be that easy. Professional help and support via rehab facilities or fellowship meetings may be required to keep clear from alcohol, drugs and other vices that people struggle with; but by keeping a regular check on what you are consuming, it can help you get a better understanding of when and how often what you are consuming will make The Shitty Committee show up.

NON-EDIBLE CONSUMPTION

SOCIAL MEDIA

Another way The Consumable Shitty Committee shows up is on what I like to call '*the weapon of mass consumption*' – also known as our digital devices. Our digital devices have helped bring us all closer together in a lot of ways, but they have also created a new way to make us feel shit about ourselves. I feel very fortunate to have grown up in an age when social media didn't exist and mobile phones were only really starting to take off. During my school years, whilst I was at the receiving end of a horrific amount of bullying at school, when I got home I was given a reprieve from the abuse. These days, abuse can come at you 24/7 through these digital devices via social media, both from people you know as well as strangers. Alongside this, the content you consume via your feeds can dictate how you feel on any one day – including happy, sad, jealous, envy, rejection, abandonment and isolation. We'll look at this in more detail in the chapter The Company You Keep but, by being aware of the type of content you are consuming and how regularly you consume it, it will either give fuel to The Shitty Committee or diminish its stranglehold on you.

WIDER MEDIA (NEWS, TV SHOWS, MAGAZINES)

The other form of The Consumable Shitty Committee that plays a significant role in how we feel about ourselves is the wider media. The media can shape our own narrative of ourselves through the news, TV shows, films, and documentaries, and the portrayal of others who we may identify with can shape the views of ourselves, be that consciously or subconsciously. An example of this was highlighted by actress Laverne Cox, who not only is an amazing actress in her own right, but an activist for the trans community. When speaking of the role the media played in her own trans journey in the documentary *Disclosure*, Cox referenced a scene in one of her favourite films growing up '*The Mask*'. She spoke of the moment where Jim Carrey's character realises another character is a transexual and goes on to projectile vomit into the toilet, creating within her a belief that people from the trans community are disgusting.

The media needs to continue to take a more proactive stance in celebrating people from all walks of life and sharing their stories, so that the future generations are able to see a part of themselves portrayed in a positive light and in influential positions. For ***You can't be what you can't see***. We, as adults, have to also be aware of what we are consuming in the media and how that is making us feel. For what we consume will shape not only our values and beliefs but the way we feel about ourselves and can often give fuel to The Shitty Committee.

Now that we've taken the time to understand the three types of The Shitty Committee, it's time to move to Section 2 of the book: When The Shitty Committee Makes You Its Slave.

SECTION 2

WHEN THE SHITTY COMMITTEE MAKES YOU ITS SLAVE

5

HOW DOES YOUR SHITTY COMMITTEE SHOW UP?

"I'm not in this world to live up to your expectations, and you are not in this world to live up to mine." – Jackie Chan

Anthony is a promising-young actor from Cardiff who, having been the lead in many of his school and regional plays growing up, made the move to London at 16 to pursue a career both in film and on the stage. He attended the prestigious Italia Conti to hone his craft and to be in London to take advantage of the many auditions and opportunities available. Anthony had always dreamed of being a leading man in a blockbuster film since seeing the likes of Dwayne Johnson and Ryan Reynolds as a little boy and, early on, those dreams seemed to be coming true as he continued to be cast as the lead. But on moving from Cardiff to London, Anthony had gone from being a big fish in a small pond, to a small fish in a vast ocean.

After securing an agent from one of the leading acting agencies, Anthony would regularly be put forward for casting calls, from West End productions and Hollywood blockbusters to television drama series and commercials. Yet as the weeks and months went by, Anthony wouldn't land any of the gigs he went for. Slowly but surely, this started to wear on Anthony as he saw several of his friends and contemporaries secure roles, and he started to question his ability to ever be cast in a leading role.

For until he moved to London, Anthony had no formal training in how to act and, as he arrived at Italia Conti, all his perceived flaws were picked out by his various teachers, from his breathing when reciting lines in a script, all the way through to his pronunciation of words when going from a Cardiff to a London to a Texan accent. To Italia Conti, Anthony was a diamond in the rough, who needed to be worked upon to bring out his star quality. However, when Anthony would receive the constructive criticism to help him improve and diversify his skill set, he would often see it as the teachers trying to dull his sparkle.

As he would attend the various casting calls to audition for the leading role, Anthony would find himself waiting in packed spaces with several other auditionees who would be reciting their lines and getting in the right frame of mind before being called in to audition for the casting directors to see them. Anthony on the other hand would be sitting there thinking '*God there are so many other talented actors here, I'm never going to stand a chance!*' or '*I just can't seem to nail this dialogue/accent/scene they want me to read for.*' After what would seem like an eternity of waiting, where those thoughts and hundreds more would build up, Anthony would nervously walk into the room, head and body closed inward, script in hand tapping away at his leg, and his confidence already tittering on a cliff edge.

As each audition would progress, thoughts in Anthony's mind would swirl round in quick succession, '*Don't fuck this up!*', '*They look so bored already and I haven't even started reciting the scene.*' and on and on they would go, blocking Anthony's ability to be fully present in the room and allowing his natural and charming personality to shine for the casting directors to see. Invariably the auditions would be short and the infamous lines '*we'll be in touch*' would be uttered as Anthony would leave the space, leaving him feeling defeated at yet another audition that he felt went terribly wrong. On his way back from the audition, thoughts would swirl in his mind saying '*Why don't you just give up this acting malarky already?*' or '*You look too fat/ugly/short to be a leading man, maybe you should settle for playing an ensemble part instead.*'

By the time Anthony had found his way to me via the trade union for creatives, Equity, he was all but ready to give up acting completely and turn his hand to another career. Over the course of a few months, I worked with Anthony to understand more about what was going on for him both at school with his teachers and throughout the audition process, to get a greater understanding of what was blocking him on the pathway towards him fulfilling his dream of becoming a leading actor. Through working together, Anthony was able to uncover that he was constantly seeking the approval of others that stemmed back to his absent father, and no matter what he did it was never good enough in his father's eyes. At school he was often bullied by other children about how he looked and so he found solace in the performing arts classes after school, where he could escape who he was and play someone else, even if only for an hour or an evening on stage when performing in shows.

All of these experiences were giving fuel to The Shitty Committee, so that when he would be faced with feedback from the teachers, he would hear his father criticising him. When he would be in a room with other auditionees, he would regress to being back in school and feeling like he didn't fit in; and as he would walk into auditions, he would be so overcome with fear that he would want to flee as soon as he possibly could. For Anthony was living in his head, where The Shitty Committee was running rife, preventing him from fulfilling his potential. Over time, Anthony was able to reconnect with why he fell in love with acting in the first place, allowing himself to sink from his head into his heart and remind himself daily of the joy he found in acting so he could stay in his heart rather than be held captive in his head by The Shitty Committee.

Ever since Anthony was able to sink from his head to his heart when auditioning and looking at the feedback from his teachers as opportunities to elevate him to a new level rather than knock him down, his performance continued to grow. He would find himself receiving call backs for auditions, which eventually led to him to land a leading part in a play on the West End stage and, three months after completing his run, Anthony auditioned and ended up being cast as one of the leading actors in a feature film.

Anthony's story is just one of a million examples of how and when The Shitty Committee shows up in someone's life, impacting their ability to live a more fulfilling life; but when The Shitty Committee shows up and how it shows up for each person is completely different. Before we take a look at your own Shitty Committee and when and how it shows up, let's first take a step back and understand more about the place where The Shitty Committee resides, in a 14cm wide by 17cm long location, weighing roughly 3lbs, otherwise known as the human brain.

According to research carried out by UCLA in Los Angeles, the average human has roughly 70,000 thoughts per day - that's a hell of a lot of thoughts right? When you break down those thoughts further into positive, negative or neutral thoughts, roughly 80 percent of them are negative, which equates to just over 69,000 negative thoughts that enter into the average human's mind every single day, or 48 negative thoughts a minute.

That's a tonne of negative thoughts for the brain to be consuming by every single day and these negative thoughts can come from a variety of different locations. One of the main sources of negativity that comes into our brains every day is the news. We have grown up in an age where negative news headlines and stories have become the go to source of content for media outlets, yet this change has only come about in the last few decades. When you look at the journey of one of the most respected news outlets, Time Magazine, in the 1950s, 90 percent of the content published was positive, but slowly over the years as the Vietnam War, the nuclear arms race, the Civil Rights Movement became front and centre of the world's attention, the lens through which Time Magazine reported these news stories started to skew into a more negative light. As this negative reporting continued to take a hold of Time Magazine, sales of the magazine continued to rise, so much that a study showed that negative headlines grabbed prospective readers' attention 30 percent more than positive headlines.

Fast forward to more recent times and, in Spring/Summer 2021, you only had to turn on the news or open up social media to quickly become overwhelmed – the rising number of deaths as a result of the ongoing Corona Virus pandemic, wars breaking out around the world, the financial crisis being faced by so many individuals, families and businesses due to the pandemic, natural disasters from flooding across Europe to earthquakes in Central America, ongoing terrorist attacks in Africa, and murders on the streets of our own cities.

The overwhelm of negative news is something I started to properly notice when I first began working in the music industry in 2001. I had the honour of working in PR for an amazing woman called Connie Filippello, who did the publicity for artists including George Michael and Mariah Carey as well as fashion houses including Versace and Tommy Hilfiger. I will always remember going through the daily press clippings of stories on our various clients and noting that so many of the stories were negative. Without missing a beat, Connie said "***If it bleeds, it leads***... dahling." Looking at a 2014 study by Outbrain around negative news headlines, it's not surprising that the study showed that the average click-through rate on negative headlines is a staggering 63 percent higher than that of their positive counterparts.

You see, if negative thoughts come into our mind 80 percent of the time, and we are attracted more to negative stories or headlines than positive ones, then the media industries are going to capitalise on this. It is a business after all and they are there to make money - not to make people happy or the world a better place. Sadly, this approach and behaviour is perpetuating a culture where The Shitty Committee residing in your own head is continuing to be fed more and more negative thoughts, which only strengthens its power within our brains to control the way we think, feel and behave.

Alongside the news, another area that can often cause The Shitty Committee to run rife is religion. Religion is a touchy subject for many, for if you criticise an individual's religion then you are criticising someone's belief system. My point here is not to criticise religion, but to highlight how religion can really give fuel to The Shitty Committee.

I have a very difficult relationship with religion. I was raised a Catholic, and Catholicism - like 72% of religions in the western world - believes that being gay is a sin, with many of those religions also believing that it is a sin punishable by death. My earliest memories as a child would be attending church each week, reading from the bible, singing along to the hymns, sometimes also attending Sunday school after mass, being baptised and christened, joining the choir and taking in all the values and beliefs that I not only read in the bible, but were shared weekly by the priest. I also attended Catholic schools throughout my childhood, further embedding the Catholic views and teachings into my mind and, though I didn't fully realise my sexuality until late into my teens, and whilst there were many positive messages that were shared in Catholicism, I had also internalised the homophobic messages from a young age, that essentially part of who I am is a sin.

These homophobic beliefs that I took in, gave The Shitty Committee all the fuel it needed to constantly tell me that who I am is wrong, disgusting, dirty, and evil, enough so that it led me to supress my sexuality even further inside of me and make me feel shame any time I let a single thought, feeling or attraction come into my mind. Religion, like the law, leads to society being governed by a set of rules and beliefs and, by and large, society conforms to these rules. Should people challenge these laws or words in the religious writings, they are often deemed outliers who are then villainised and ostracised even further by society. Over the past hundred or so years, many of those who were villainised, have helped us to take massive steps forward in the fight for equality, from the suffragette movement in 1918, giving women the right to vote through to the civil rights movement in America in the 1960s, leading to the Civil Rights Act of 1964, which outlawed discrimination based on race, colour, religion, sex and national origin. Yet despite all the advances in these areas, racism, sexism, homophobia, classism and more still run rife around the world, as views and beliefs continue to get passed down from generation to generation. And so, even if a law is changed, a deeply held view or belief continues to be held strongly and passed from a parent to a child, unless somewhere along the way the pattern is interrupted and broken.

Another way that The Shitty Committee can grow inside of you can be from your parents and primary caregivers who, whilst often doing the best they can with the knowledge and resources they have, are passing on their own negative values and beliefs they have carried within themselves, owning to what they were exposed to growing up. For trauma and negative beliefs that are not treated are transmitted on to subsequent generations. They may have a bad relationship with money due to growing up in a recession or their parents being bad with their finances, so they have projected that on to you. This may fuel The Shitty Committee to say things like '*Why are you wasting your money on X or Y when you should be saving every penny you can?*', when you are actually investing in yourself to provide a better future. They may have come from a period of instability in their careers or their own parents' careers, so they believe it is important to be employed rather than self-employed because it offers more stability and a regular pay-check. Again, their limiting beliefs are being projected onto you, which then shows up in The Shitty Committee as '*Why are you going to leave your full time job with its regular salary, to take a chance on a half-baked idea that's destined to fail?*', when actually you are taking massive action by building that idea into a plan to help bring that new business opportunity to life and create a pathway to a more fulfilling life.

Friends, teachers, employers can all come with their own negative values and beliefs that they project on to you too, helping to further add to the arsenal of lines The Shitty Committee can use to stop you from living a more fulfilling life, to prevent you from taking uncomfortable action to level up, to keep you as its slave.

You see The Shitty Committee is an amalgamation of all those different people who have entered into your life at different points who, whether intentionally or unintentionally, have shared values and beliefs that you have internalised. The Shitty Committee has weaponised these against you to make you play safe and to prevent you from stepping outside your comfort zone towards a more fulfilling life. To understand how The Shitty Committee shows up for you, what I want you to do now is go through each area below and on the next page and start to make an inventory of all the values and beliefs that you have taken on from any area of your life that has impacted the way you think, look of feel about yourself.

Parents or Primary Caregivers

____

____

____

____

Siblings

____

____

____

____

Friends

____

____

____

____

Bullies

____

____

____

____

Bosses / Work Colleagues

Religion

Media

The Law

Teachers

Others

Now you have done that, I want you to go back through each and every one of the things you've listed with a fine-tooth comb and think, how is that serving me today? Some of the values and beliefs that The Shitty Committee has taken on from others have helped us to make it through our childhoods. For example, if your parents said '*Children should be seen and not heard*', The Shitty Committee will have internalised that as '*What you say doesn't matter*' or '*You better keep your mouth shut or you'll get into trouble.*' During childhood, The Shitty Committee actually may have been helping you, as if you did speak out you may have been at the receiving end of verbal, physical, emotional or even sexual abuse from your parents, but as you grew older and became an adult, you lost your voice and never felt comfortable speaking out when something didn't sit right with you, leading you to do things you didn't want to do and taking you further away from living a more fulfilling life and actualising your full potential.

Most, if not all, of the things on your list will no longer be serving you and, in later chapters, we will look at ways you can master The Shitty Committee so that you are no longer held captive by the things written above, allowing you to stop feeling like shit and start to move forward towards a more fulfilling life. Before we do that, I want to take a moment to honour the old version of you that's missed out on life – the version of you that allowed The Shitty Committee to control your life and prevent you from fulfilling your full potential. I want you to take a moment to write down all the things The Shitty Committee has prevented you from doing in your life, whether it be going for that promotion, asking that person out on a date, starting that business you've always wanted to launch or anything else that comes to mind. Write it down below and, if you need to, go ahead and grab some additional paper, or use the additional blank lined pages in Index 2, to write down your thoughts. I have a feeling you may have a few things to write down!

Now that you've highlighted all the times in the past The Shitty Committee has prevented you from achieving your full potential and living a more fulfilling life, I want you to identify if there a specific period of time that The Shitty Committee shows up. For some people, it may turn up all the time without a care for timings, but usually it prefers to turn up more frequently at one time or place over all others, because it likes familiarity. It could be in the mornings when The Shitty Committee starts to go through all the things you have ahead or did the night before; it could be late at night just as you're going to bed that The Shitty Committee has time to finally be heard as you've been too busy to notice it. The Shitty Committee could show up only in social settings. So when is that time for you? Write it down below if you know and, if you don't, monitor it over the next week and see if a pattern emerges. You can come back to this later and write it below if so.

I appreciate there is a lot of work you are putting in here and it can be quite exhausting emotionally to look back at all the ways The Shitty Committee shows up and what it has prevented you from doing so far in your life. I commend you for continuing to put yourself first and encourage you to persevere through this chapter so you can expose how and when The Shitty Committee shows up in your life.

Before we move onto the next chapter, I want you to use this next page in the book to first write down all things, you are no longer willing to accept from The Shitty Committee in your life. Then, I want you to write down all the things that are now musts in your life, so that you can go on to live a more fulfilling life.

Things I am no longer willing to accept in my life
(*e.g. negative influences, being broke etc*)

Things that are now musts in my life
(*e.g. Following my passion, changing career*)

Take a look at that list for a moment and, in the list of musts, check to see if there is anything that is missing from that list of that needs to be added to help you live a more fulfilling life. Is it that you must start putting yourself first? Is it that you must start making time to put a business plan together to start the process of launching your business? If anything comes up, add it to your list.

Next, revisit the list of things you are no longer willing to accept in your life, to see if there is anything else that is going to stop you from fulfilling your full potential. Are you no longer going to accept people's advice who have no experience or knowledge of where you want to go? Is it that you are no longer willing to accept some of the stories The Shitty Committee tells you that keep holding you back from achieving your full potential? Whatever else comes up, jot it down now.

Well done, you've put a lot of effort into this chapter and, before we move on to the next to look at The Company You Keep, I want you to take a moment to savour the work you have put in and reward yourself. It doesn't have to be anything big - it can be anything from a nice hot bath, to doing something creative like painting or origami. Whatever you decide make the time before you start the next chapter to acknowledge how you are taking massive action to help yourself live a more fulfilling life. How you are strengthening your inner goddess or superhero to take on The Shitty Committee. Through identifying all the things The Shitty Committee says, how they no longer serve you, how you will no longer allow it to hold you back and the first steps you must take, you are well on the pathway to living a more fulfilling life.

6

THE COMPANY YOU KEEP

"Small minds discuss people. Average minds discuss events. Great minds discuss ideas." – Eleanor Roosevelt

"Don't downgrade your dream to fit your reality, upgrade your conviction to match your destiny." – Stuart W Scott

There once was a young girl named Ella who lived happily in a large house with her parents along with a few servants, until one day her mother fell seriously ill. It was a short illness that would take Ella's mum's life and, upon her deathbed, Ella made a promise to keep her mum's wish to always have courage and to be kind. Several years later, Ella's father went on to marry a recently widowed woman named Lady Tremaine, moving into Ella's family home and also bringing into the family two unpleasant step-sisters, Drizella and Anastasia.

As time passes, whilst Ella's dad is away on business, Lady Tremaine starts to reveal her cruel and jealous nature, forcing Ella to give up her bedroom to her stepsisters and move up into the attic. Later still, when Ella's dad unexpectedly dies, Lady Tremaine gets rid of all the servants to save money, forcing all of their tasks onto Ella alone, leaving her step-mum and step-sisters to continue living a life of luxury and Ella without either of her parents or someone to love and care for her.

One day, distraught over the treatment from her stepfamily, Ella flees the house and rides off into the woods where she encounters the Crown Prince out hunting. Unaware that he is a Prince, both Ella and Kit (the crown-prince) take a shine to each other, but they part without Kit learning her name. Kit's father discovering he doesn't have long left to live, urges Kit to take a Princess as his bride at the upcoming royal ball. Desperate to reconnect with the woman he met in the woods, Kit persuades his father to invite every eligible woman in the kingdom, hoping to see Ella once more.

As her stepfamily prepares to leave for the ball, Ella attempts to join them so she can meet Kit once more, wearing a re-imagined dress from her late mum. Lady Tremaine and her daughters laugh at the preposterous idea that their now servant would get to attend the ball and destroy the dress, leaving Ella behind as they head off for the evening. Heartbroken by the repeated cruel treatment of her step-mum and stepsisters, Ella runs out to the garden in tears where she meets an old beggar woman who reveals herself to be Ella's godmother. Ella's godmother transforms Ella's ripped dress into a beautiful ball gown and gives her a pair of glass slippers to match, whilst also providing transport for her to the ball, using magic to turn a pumpkin into a carriage, mice into horses and a final spell to ensure her stepfamily don't recognise her, but her godmother warns Ella that the magic will end before the last stroke of midnight. Arriving at the ball, Kit is delighted to see Ella once more and they share the first dance together, where Ella comes to learns that Kit is actually the Crown Prince and not a palace apprentice.

Just as they get to know each other more, the clock strikes midnight and Ella flees the palace without revealing her name; and in a rush to get back before the spell wears off, she loses one of her glass slippers. Kit, having already lost Ella once in the woods, was determined not to lose Ella again and so sets out to find her, professing his love for the mystery Princess, requesting she present herself to him. Ella, on hearing the news, rushes to retrieve her other glass slipper with a dream of finally being free from the clutches of her evil stepfamily, but Lady Tremaine has found the other glass slipper first and says she will only allow Ella to marry the Prince on the condition that she make her head of the royal household and find husbands for her stepsisters. Ella, sick of the treatment at the hands of her stepmother, refuses and so Lady Tremaine smashes the glass slipper to pieces and locks Ella in the attic, dashing her chances of ever being reconnected with the Prince.

The Prince, however, doesn't give up hope and goes from household to household in an attempt to find the mystery princess whose foot fits the slipper; but it refuses to fit anyone. Upon arrival at Ella's house, the shoe fits neither step-sister, but just as the search team go to leave the house they hear Ella singing and Kit demands them to find where the sound is coming from. Ella is released from the attic and, when trying on the slipper, it fits Ella perfectly. Finally, both knowing one another's true identity, Kit and Ella promise to accept one another for who they truly are, and as they leave to make their way to the palace, Ella forgives her step-mother for everything she put her through. Ella and Kit go on to marry and become the Kingdom's most beloved monarchs, ruling with the same courage and kindness that Ella had promised her mother.

Ella, more commonly known as Cinderella, is one of the oldest known fairy tales of all time and the story helps to highlight how the company you keep can have an impact on the way The External Shitty Committee can make you feel. For Ella lived in a beloved family who made her feel loved and special until her parents died, wherein the company she was then forced to keep made her into a servant, treating her horribly and at every turn trying to prevent her from living a more fulfilling life. Despite their attempts to dull her sparkle, Ella clung to the words that her late mother had said to be courageous and kind, and as she met the Prince and her Godmother, her diminishing faith was once again lit; there could be a brighter future for her. As that faith became a reality, she went on to live a more fulfilling life (or as it goes in Disney films, happily ever after).

Similar to Cinderella's story, we as humans also require a sense of belonging to someone who loves us, for it is an essential need for our existence. Feeling like you belong somewhere means that you matter, whether that is to someone or something, and when you matter you have a driving force to get you through the good times and the hard times; and the thing that most helps you feel like you belong is the company you keep.

Whether you call them your tribe, your gang, your family, your crew, your friends, your colleagues or something else, all these different groups form those who are closest to you and, out of the 7.8 billion people that currently live on this planet, only the smallest of percentiles ever enter your orbit. British evolutionary anthropologist Robin Dunbar was fascinated by the human population and their relationship with one another and so he set out to research how humans interact with each other across history, to find patterns that could help inform what the optimum number of people is for a person to not only know everyone but to create a sense of belonging.

When he looked at the Neolithic farming communities (our great great ancestors) he saw that these communities would reach a cap of roughly 150 people before they would split off into a separate community, so that no farming community reached more than 150. When he looked at the Roman military armies, they would be approximately 150 people in size, ensuring that the General would be able to know every member of their Division, which still continues through to modern day armies which vary between 120 and 180 per Regiment. As Dunbar continued his research, he saw that smaller subsets within the magic number of 150 emerged, from looking at the average number of players on a sports team to the average number of students in a class and the number of people that form a jury. In his findings, Dunbar came up with the numbers below that formed his thinking around the company we keep. Dunbar believed we have:

- 5 intimate friends
- 15 good friends (including the 5 intimate friends)

- 50 friends (including the 5 intimate friends and 10 good friends) and
- 150 acquaintances

Now Dunbar came up with these numbers in the early 1990s just as the dawn of the digital era was setting in and, when looking back at a lot of his research, though the core components still stand, it was based primarily on communities that spent their whole lives near each other. In today's age, with technology advancing so that we can travel to the other side of the world in less than a day and can live in the most remote part of the world and still connect with people through a digital device, the social network of humans has now expanded to where, on social media platforms, the average number of followers, friends, subscribers a person has is 338.

As such, Dunbar's numbers have been expanded to take this into consideration and we now have a new model that is more reflective of the current world we live in. It is believed that the average individual's network has:

No of People.	Type of Network	Explanation of Network
5	Inner Circle	Our tightest circle of loved ones, which we devote around 40% of our social time too.
15	Sympathy Group	These are our good friends. On average we devote an additional 20% of our social time to the additional 10 people in this category.
50	Close Network	A further 35 friends are added into the mix.
150	Personal Network	The average brain limit for meaningful relationships
500	Acquaintances	People we have contact with but the additional 350 people are not part of our core network.
1,500	Recognisable People	Faces we recognise but people we don't have a great deal of social contact with.

Figure 1 - Your Personal Network

When looking at the research above and the amount of time we devote to those in our inner circle (40%), if you want to get to know someone, speak with the five people closest to them and you will have a good sense of who they are, from what interests they have, to what their views are, and what station they are at in their life.

You see, as we grow through life, the individuals that form our inner circle will evolve and change. When we are infants, our inner circle is likely to consist of our parents or primary caregivers, our siblings if we have any, and a friend or two. As we continue to grow up, our inner circle will evolve with some people still staying in our inner circle, whilst others start to move to the outer circles. Think about some of the friends you had at primary school. Some of them will have been your best friends and part of your inner circle, but as you moved to secondary school, they may have gone to a different school than you and, as such, they aren't in your orbit as frequently, and so your friendship evolves or devolves; they slowly move to your sympathy group as you see them less and, as time passes, they move further and further out to the point where, down the road, you may have got a friend request on social media from said friend you haven't seen in 20+ years that, whilst you recognise, you haven't had any social contact with.

A person you used to be married to will have been part of your inner circle but, since your divorce, depending on how amicable it was and whether you co-parent or not, they are likely to move to one of the outer circles. A friend you used to go out partying with may no longer be in your inner circle now that you have decided to live a sober life or may have settled down with children, whilst you remain single. Relationships evolve as people grow and change, and certain people who used to serve our needs may no longer do so.

As the expression goes, there are three types of people:

1. People in your life for a reason
2. People in your life for a season
3. People in your life for a lifetime

At the time that person enters our lives, we may not know which of the three categories they fall into but, over time, if we pay close enough attention, we will come to notice which one they fall into. Are they a person that has been brought into our lives for a reason to teach us a valuable lesson? Are they someone that will be with us for a season as we go through a certain period of our lives, education, business, or relocation? Or are they someone who will be with us for a lifetime through the good times and the hard times?

Sometimes it can be hard to tell; like a hotel, when people leave long after the designated check-out time impacting newly arriving guests checking in, certain people in our lives outstay their welcome, which also prevents new people from entering our lives. Think of a romantic relationship - every day you stay in that relationship with someone you are no longer in love with, you miss the opportunity to enter into a new relationship with someone who is more deserving of your time and love.

So how does all of this relate to The Shitty Committee and living a more fulfilling life? As mentioned previously, you are a reflection of the five people closest to you. Who they are and how they are with you will have a significant impact on how you feel and how fulfilled you are in your life. So before we move forward, I want you to note down the five people that form your inner circle:

1. ______________________________
2. ______________________________
3. ______________________________
4. ______________________________
5. ______________________________

For each and every person, the five people that occupy the above list is going to be different, not only because we all know different people, but because we are all at different stations in our lives and therefore the five people that occupy these slots are there to fulfil a certain need within us. Also, at least one of the people that occupied your inner circle three years ago is not likely to appear above in the five people closest to you today.

The next thing I want you to do is think of the area/s wherein you want to live a more fulfilling life. Do you want to be financially secure for the rest of your life? Do you want to be in a committed and healthy relationship? Do you want to achieve your ideal weight? Do you want to become a successful entrepreneur? Whatever it is that you want to lead a more fulfilling life, write it down below.

____

____

____

____

What I want you to do next is to look through the area/s you've just written down in which you want to live a more fulfilling life, and then look at the five people that form your inner circle to see who on that list is able to help you achieve those goals, but before you do that, I just want you to think about this. If one of your goals is to live a financially fulfilling life, would you go to Broke Ass Bob who is always in debt for advice? If you want to become a successful entrepreneur, would you go to Pessimist Pete who always looks at the negatives in life and has no business experience? I don't think you would. So go back now and check through your list and see who on your list is able to help you live a more fulfilling life in the area/s you've highlighted.

There's a great expression that the actor Morgan Freeman put on my radar that states:

'Don't take criticism from people you wouldn't go to for advice.'

This is an important expression to remember. We can often let criticism from others, who have no business giving us advice on a certain area or subject, give fuel to The Shitty Committee, which then talks us out of what we want to do and prevents us from living a more fulfilling life. Do any of the people in your inner circle help in your quest to live a more fulfilling life? If yes, then that's amazing and, if not, then not to worry, this is where we are here to help. Back in the 20th Century, in most industries, it used to be what you know that would get you in the door, but nowadays, irrespective of the industry you wish to enter, it is not what you know but who you know that will get you ahead in life. And this equally applies to you on your quest to live a more fulfilling life, for:

Your Network = Your Net Worth

We'll be going into more detail on this in the next chapter, Becoming A Gynaecologist, but just to stay with this area a little more before we do so, I want you to look at your list on page 57 and identify how many people in your inner circle are taking up space and time (remember those in your inner circle you spend up to 40% of your social time with), that whilst they may contribute to your life in certain ways, they may not able to contribute to you living a more fulfilling life in the area/s you listed.

If you have identified at least one or more spaces, I want you to identify either the person you need (if you already know them or know of them) or the type of person you need that will help you to lead a more fulfilling life. And remember if, for example, you want to become a successful entrepreneur, you may want a successful entrepreneur as one of the five closest people to you. Whilst one of the five people currently in your inner circle may have no experience in entrepreneurship, they may be your biggest cheerleader and rightfully deserve to stay in your inner circle, as they can be your shoulder to cry on when you hit an obstacle, a motivational force when experiencing a turbulent patch, in addition to that successful entrepreneur that can offer insight and guidance. Your inner circle should be formed not only of people that add knowledge, skills and expertise to fulfil your full potential, but those who also add emotional and spiritual support. If you need to evolve your inner circle, use the spaces below to list your new inner circle highlighting the changes you will make.

1. ________________________________
2. ________________________________
3. ________________________________
4. ________________________________
5. ________________________________

In the next chapter, Becoming A Gynaecologist, we are going to look in more detail at the people who currently occupy your close network, sympathy group and inner circle but, in closing, I want you to think about whether there is someone currently in your inner circle who doesn't contribute to you living a more fulfilling life. They may be someone who hasn't made your evolved inner circle list, and it may be time to look at which space they should be occupying in your life. Could they move out one ring to your sympathy group, so they are still there to support you but not intimately involved in your process, or should they be moved much further out to your acquaintances group or potentially recognisable people because they are no longer serving you but in fact hindering you in living a more fulfilled life?

Only you can make that decision and, in Chapter 9, The Pain In The (Secondary) Gains, we will explore why some people may be harder to move out from our inner circle than others. For now, let's continue to focus on how to get you to live a more fulfilled life by becoming a gynaecologist.

7

BECOMING A GYNAECOLOGIST

"Once you start seeing your worth, you'll find it harder to stick around those who don't.'" – Unknown

"Never let another person close the curtains on your window of opportunity." – Jack Williamson

Back at the start of January in 2008, I packed up all my earthly belongings and left London for Los Angeles. Excited to embark on the next chapter of my career, I'd been offered an opportunity to go and work for an artist management company. I'd been let go from my role in International Marketing at EMI Records, due to a period of cost cutting measures following the collapse of the music industry in the wake of Napster, which saw 50% of the entire value of the global recorded music industry wiped away.

Unlike many people who go to Los Angeles or, more specifically, Hollywood with dreams to make it as a star, I've never really been interested in being someone in front of the camera and, having worked alongside so many artists, I've witnessed first-hand the negative impact that fame and success in that field can bring. But I was new to the city and, apart from my new boss who I was going to work for, a couple of artists I worked with in my career and Ginger, who I'd met on a previous trip, I didn't know anyone in Los Angeles.

Truth be told, it was quite a lonely period the first few months as I tried to find my bearings in a new city and build up a social circle. Ginger proved to be an amazing foundation in helping me build a social circle, as her parents, siblings, nieces, nephews and daughter welcomed me into their family, shining a light not only on how much of a beautiful soul Ginger has but the importance of a solid base and family to help get you through both the good times and hard times.

I'd arguably say that there is no place this is more needed than in Los Angeles. You need, what I call, those radiators in your life - the people who fill you up with love, warmth and energy - because on every corner, no matter where you go there are, what I call, drains nearby, that is those people who suck every ounce of your energy from you. I noticed this the first time I got invited to a Hollywood party. It was like one of those parties you see in the movies where everyone looks beautiful, set in an amazing venue and I felt completely out of place. To try and make myself more comfortable I headed to the bar for some Dutch courage and as I was waiting for the bartender to make my drink, a guy came up alongside me and says '*Hey nice to meet you, what do you do?*' Confused, thinking I missed him asking for my name, I said '*I'm Jack nice to meet you, what's your name?*' which then opened up into a monologue about who he was, how he came to Hollywood to be an actor and has starred in many different shows, and is just about to land the lead in a big motion picture film. After a few more pleasantries, he was off to circle the room, finding the next victim who would be filled with his monologue, after realising that I couldn't further his ambitions to be a film star.

As the night wore on, I came to realise that apart from the person themselves, the conversations that occurred with others that night followed pretty much the same pattern, where they didn't ask for your name, they cut straight to the chase, asking you what you do, to evaluate whether you were an asset they could use to further their career ambitions, or a liability who, in their eyes, viewed you as not worthy of their time. I went into the night full of energy with what I hoped would be an opportunity to meet new people, expand my network and hopefully make new friends, but instead it left me at the end of the night feeling completely drained and not wanting to go to another Hollywood party again. As I drove back to my house, I sat there thinking to myself about some of the people that I met and wondered:

Did they get a call from NASA telling them the world revolves around them and not the sun?

This type of person isn't unique to Hollywood and they can be found no matter where you are in the world. Heck, I'm sure you have at least one friend you can think of right now who, whenever you are with them, the conversation always tends to revolve around them, leaving little to no space for you to share what's going on with you. Those people often come away from that time with you feeling better about themselves and think they have a great relationship with you and how you are so supportive and understanding and know exactly what to say but, in truth, the relationship is very one sided as you are left on the other side, always listening to their latest news, problems, celebrations or issues. They show little to no concern about you, or what you may be going through, your successes you may want to celebrate, or your struggles you need help in overcoming.

As humans, we have four main communication styles and, whilst radiators (which we will touch upon later in this chapter) generally spend most of their time in the first quadrant, drains spend nearly all their time in the other three. The four quadrants are:

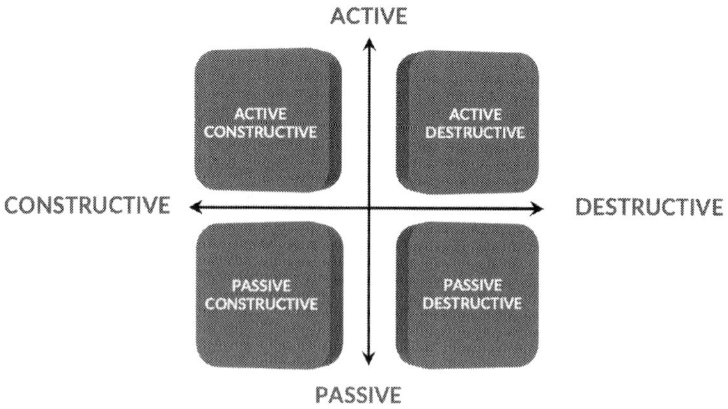

Figure 2 - The Four Types Of Communication

ACTIVE CONSTRUCTIVE

Active Constructive communication occurs when you are having a conversation with another person and they or you are actively engaged in acknowledging what is being said, expressing a real interest in what is being discussed, and asking follow-up questions to really understand more about what is going on.

ACTIVE DESTRUCTIVE

Active Destructive communication occurs when you are having a conversation with someone about something (for example, a recent break-up that has affected you) and, whatever it is you are talking about, they turn it into a conversation about themselves, usually related to a similar experience they've had (for example, how their break-up was so much worse) and not making any effort to check in on you, leaving you not able to talk to them about what is going on.

PASSIVE CONSTRUCTIVE

Passive Constructive communication occurs very frequently in the digital age where, when having a conversation with someone, they are half-way in the conversation but they are also pre-occupied doing something else too (be it watching TV, on their phones, cooking), thus not granting you their full attention.

PASSIVE DESTRUCTIVE

Passive Destructive communication occurs when you bring up a topic of conversation to someone and they just completely ignore what has been said and switch the conversation to something else, for example '*what's for dinner?*', leaving you feeling like what you have to say doesn't matter, robbing you of your joy or compounding your sadness.

Whilst we can all fall into each of these communication styles from time to time, the drains in our lives will generally fall more frequently onto the right side of the four quadrants. By getting to know an individual's primary communication style, we can become more aware of those kinds of people who are drains in our life and who leave us often feeling worse after being with them. That way we can start to look at how we can keep those drains at bay.

Drains not only have different communication styles but can show up in different guises too. There are six main types of drains which are:

1. The Energy Vampire
2. The Pessimist
3. The Liar
4. The Manipulator
5. The Victim
6. The Instigator

On the next two pages are further details on each of the six different types of drains that can come into your life, that can stop you on the pathway to a more fulfilling life.

THE ENERGY VAMPIRE

The Energy Vampire is that person in your life who sucks the energy out of a room. By needing to be the centre of attention, they drain you of all your energy, usually emotionally but often physically too. They use the energy that you give them by being a supportive friend to fill them up, but disregard you once they've got what they want.

THE PESSIMIST

The Pessimist, or as I like to refer to them, the Debbie Downer is that person in your life that always looks at things through a negative lens. When something goes their way or your way, rather than celebrating all that it took to achieve it, they just say they/you were lucky or, rather than focusing on all the things that could go right, they spend their time solely focusing on everything that could go wrong.

THE LIAR

The Liar is that person in your life that will come up with falsehoods or alternative facts and often shows up most in romantic relationships talking about where they've been, what they've been up to, and why they haven't done things they said they were going to do. They can also show up in business relationships, lying about similar stories and leaving you feeling drained because you've had to pick up the slack for the weight they're not pulling.

THE MANIPULATOR

The manipulator is not too dissimilar to the victim, though they can vary. The manipulator is skilled at convincing you to do things you don't want to do or in bringing you around to their way of thinking, making you abandon your own thoughts or logic. They also are skilled at turning everything around and placing blame on others, rather than accepting their role in the situation.

THE VICTIM

The Victim is that person in your life who never takes responsibility or accountability for their actions and places the blame on you/others (making you or others the persecutor), leaving you in a position to either stay as the persecutor or become the rescuer who is always attempting to help them through whatever situation they find themselves in. Now don't get me wrong, there are many people in life who are victim to some seriously traumatic events, but as the expression that we previously shared at the start of this book goes:

Your Trauma Isn't Your Fault, But Your Healing Is Your Responsibility.

Those who always live in their victimhood can be extreme drains on your energy if you continue to give a significant amount of your time to them.

THE INSTIGATOR

The Instigator is always that individual who starts the drama, whether it be picking a fight or causing a scene; they are the ones who stir the pot and then step back to watch the drama unfold, leaving others to clean up the mess that they helped to create.

I'm sure as you were reading through the various types of drains, different people from your life were coming to mind that you could instantly recognise as having that quality, or potentially more than one of those qualities. If you want to live a more fulfilling life, you need to keep those drains at bay so they don't give fuel to The Shitty Committee. By switching out those drains for radiators you are going to increase your positive emotions. As we explored in the previous chapter, those that fill your inner circle or sympathy group take up nearly two-thirds of your time (60%). If most of those five to fifteen people that fill those circles are drains, that is going to form not only a really strong External Shitty Committee to make you feel shit about yourself, but also provide fuel for your Internal Shitty Committee, to replay the negative thoughts that they share to stop you achieving your full potential.

It is important therefore, that you create an environment that allows you to grow and live a more fulfilling life, rather than stay in an environment that makes you feel like shit and keeps you stuck I love the following analogy that really helps to embed this point. *A shark in a fish tank will grow 8 inches, but in the ocean, it will grow to 8 feet or more. The shark will never outgrow its environment and the same is true about you.* Many times, we're around small thinking people and so we don't grow. Change your environment and watch your growth.

To do this, I like to use, what I call, Becoming A Gynaecologist Model - a 3-step approach for dealing with the drains in your life.

DISCLAIMER ALERT

If you are not a fan of the C word, then you should jump forward to page 72. However I encourage you to be comfortable in your uncomfortableness with this word, as this section will really help you to master The Shitty Committee.

You see, drains can also be referred to as Cunts and too many cunts in your life can leave you feeling Cunstipated. What does Cunstipated mean I hear you say. Well, here is a definition for you:

. . .

CUNSTIPATED – *an emotional or spiritual blockage caused by having to deal with too many cunts in one day.*

When you spend your time around too many cunts, they impact both your emotions and your spirit (which we will talk about more in Chapter 10 - That's The Spirit). They make you feel shit about yourself, questioning your hopes, dreams and aspirations as pie in the sky ideas that will never come to fruition, all the way through to pushing you down in front of others so it raises them up to look better. They come with thoughts, views and beliefs that will slowly but surely diminish your hopes and dreams. You might not notice to begin with but, over time, they will build and build and eventually something that one of those cunts say will become the straw that breaks the camel's back. This leaves you abandoning your hopes and dreams, not fulfilling your potential, and keeping you trapped in the same environment you are trying to grow out of.

This is why I want you to become gynaecologists, because they can spot a cunt a mile away! And if you have that skill set too, you can then make a proactive decision to not allow them to enter your inner circle or sympathy circle so that you don't end up feeling Cunstipated. This will allow your emotional and spiritual energy to flourish by surrounding yourself with radiators who will help to propel you forward to fulfilling your full potential. The 3-steps to Becoming A Gynaecologist are as follows:

STEP 1

What I want you to do is to write down a list of anyone who makes you feel cunstipated in any area of your life. It's important when doing this exercise to think of people who make you feel cunstipated in all areas of your life. If, for example, you want to fulfil your full potential in your current place of work and climb up the corporate ladder, it may be that your boss or a colleague are the drains that makes you feel cunstipated and so they would be two people who would make the list. But you may also have a friend or partner outside of work who makes you feel cunstipated and depletes your energy levels to a point that it causes a knock on effect in your work, where you don't have the energy to work on that project which is going to get you that promotion to allow you to live a more fulfilling life.

Below, make a list of anyone in your life who makes you feel Cunstipated:

1. ______________________________
2. ______________________________
3. ______________________________
4. ______________________________
5. ______________________________
6. ______________________________
7. ______________________________
8. ______________________________
9. ______________________________
10. ______________________________

STEP 2

Next to each of these names, I want you to identify where they sit within your social network and put the following initials next to them to denote which zone they are in: IC (Inner Circle), SG (Sympathy Group), CN (Close Network), PN (Personal Network), A (Acquaintances) or RP (Recognisable People) – if you can't recall the breakdown of what each zone means turn back to page 55. If any of these people have an IC, SG or CN besides their name, you need to single those individuals out and identify how much time you spend with them in an average week (be that in person, on calls, or via written communication) and add the total number of hours up.

Once you've come up with that number, I want you to do a little maths here (feel free to use a calculator if you need to). Take your total number of hours, divide it by 168 (the number of hours in a week) and then times it by 100. For example:

24 (hours with people that make me feel cunstipated) ÷ 168 = 0.1428 x 100 = 14.28%

That calculation will give you the percentage of time each week that you spend with people who make you feel cunstipated, blocking your emotional and spiritual energy, and preventing you from living a more fulfilling life. So now it's your turn:

______ ÷ 168 = ______ x 100 = ______ %

No matter what percentage your answers came out with, the main point here is that your time is precious if you want to fulfil your full potential and, if any of these drains who make you feel cunstipated are in your inner circle, sympathy group or close network, you are giving permission for The External Shitty Committee to live rent free inside your head. No matter how small or insignificant it may seem, they will put roadblocks on your pathway to living a more fulfilling life.

I can already hear some people's Internal Shitty Committee shouting out to me with stories like 'but Jack you don't understand I look after my sick father and he is one of the people who makes me feel cunstipated' and I honour that - I truly do. For many of us have responsibilities in our lives that mean that those who make us feel cunstipated are also the ones who most need our help. I'm not asking you to remove them from your life, I am asking you to first identify the amount of time you give to those who make you feel cunstipated before we move on to the final step.

STEP 3

Now that you have identified all the people that make you feel cunstipated, where they lie in your social network and how much time, on average, they collectively take up each week, the final step is to identify what to do with them.

As mentioned in Step 2, you may be responsible for the health and well-being of some of those people and we will come back to those in a second. But for those who are not your responsibility, it's time to get ruthless and remove them from your inner circle, sympathy group or close network, for they are no longer serving you but hindering you on your pathway to fulfilling your full potential. It will be easier for some than for others, because they may be islands on their own as opposed to members of a group you are close to; but no matter how easy or hard it is in removing them from those three circles, if you want to live a more fulfilling life then you need to take uncomfortable action.

This may result, in some instances, in having to burn bridges completely with certain individuals who don't want to fall back to one of your outer circles i.e. the personal network, acquaintances or recognisable people and, if this is the case, then remember:

May the bridges I burn light a way to a brighter future

I get it, it will be hard to let some of them go and we will look at that more in the next chapter. But trust me when I say this, when you remove those drains who make you feel cunstipated from your life, you will flourish and thrive in ways you never imagined were possible before. And for those of you who have someone who is dependent on you, whilst you can't change them, you can change how you engage with them. For example, take the time to think of ways you can meet your commitments whilst reducing time with them (i.e. blocking out me time). Additionally choose not to share with them how you are going to live a more fulfilling life, if you know they will shoot it down. Making these small adjustments, and others you can think of, will help reduce their ability to make you feel like shit, whilst also increasing your ability to continue focusing on moving towards a more fulfilling life.

We've spent the majority of this chapter focusing on the drains in your life, but I want to take a moment to do a shout out to all the radiators in your life. Radiators, as mentioned before, are those people who fill you up, and make you feel warmer inside when you are with them and long after you part from them. They are the people who are there for you through the good times and the hard times. They are not the ones you call to bail you out if you find yourself sitting in jail after a raucous night out; they are the ones sitting next to you laughing at how you both got into this mess and working with you to find a way out of it.

And when I say jail, I'm talking metaphorically, not literally. They are the ones who know the paths you have travelled because they've been on the journey with you, helping to lift you up when you are down, cheering you on from the side-lines as you move forward in the right direction, and helping you to think outside the box to harness those ideas and turn them into plans of action - ***for an idea without a plan is just a dream***. Radiators may also be people who aren't in your inner circle, sympathy group or close network, but they still radiate positivity, energy and more into your life. For me, those people include Oprah Winfrey, Tony Robbins and Dean Graziosi, and ,who knows, one day they may even move into one of my inner circles.

As we come towards the end of this chapter, I want you to identify all the radiators in your life and write them down below (remember they can both be someone you know like a friend, or someone you don't know yet, like a public figure, podcaster or author):

1. ______________________
2. ______________________
3. ______________________
4. ______________________
5. ______________________
6. ______________________
7. ______________________
8. ______________________
9. ______________________
10. ______________________

From there, I want you to identify how much time you get to

spend with each of them on an average week and write it next to each of their names. If, like me, there are radiators in your life who you don't currently have access to in terms of communicating directly with them, then how much time you spend consuming material from them that fills you up and can help you on the pathway to fulfilling your full potential?

You can calculate the percentage of time you spend with the radiators in your life each week using the same calculation you did with the drains:

_______ ÷ 168 = _______ x 100 = ______ %

Hopefully the total in your radiators is more than your drains but, if not, don't worry - you are in the process of removing those people from your inner circle/sympathy group/close network and clearing the way for more radiators to take those spots. The goal here is not to get as high a percentage as possible, - on average, most humans spend a third of their life sleeping, so the highest you are going to get is 66.6% in the radiator section if you only spend your time around radiators. Even then, you will still need some 'me time' to focus on you. We can spend all our time looking outside to get filled up, but it is when we spend time with ourselves and look inside that we truly awaken to our full potential. That time on our own really helps us build on the support of our radiators to fulfil our full potential and live a more fulfilling life.

An ideal amount of time to be spending with radiators is between 25%-33%, and with drains as little time as possible, ideally a ratio of 1:10 in terms of time compared to being with the radiators. The rest of your time should be spent on focusing on yourself and sleeping, to build up your energy to take on each and every day as it comes.

One final thought around radiators and drains I want to leave you with before we move onto the next chapter is about your social media/media consumption.

Social media has become the primary method through which many people now communicate with others, with over 80% of the adult population of the Western world on at least one social media platform. Whilst social media has opened the door to new ways in which to communicate and new opportunities for people to find others with similar interests to their own, more than one in three adults (38%) see social media use as harmful, with only 5% seeing it as positive.

Statistics comparing the rise of social media with the mental health of children and adolescents shows worrying concerns too. Since 2010, child suicide rates have increased by up to 150% and self-harm by girls aged 10 to 14 have nearly tripled. Adolescents in Year 8 (12-13 year olds) who spend over 10 hours a week on social media are 56% more likely to report being unhappy than those who spend less time on social media, and whilst these figures are staggering and relate only to children, similar impacts are being seen in adults too.

We have even seen many public figures including the likes of Ed Sheeran and Justin Bieber taking a break from social media to protect their mental health. Social media can not only make you feel worse by seeing what other people are doing and comparing their highlight reel to your real life, but you can also be on the receiving end of cyber-bullying both by people who you may know and also by trolls you've never met before. This all gives fuel to The Shitty Committee and so to help you live a more fulfilling life, take a look at your social media, look through your feeds and all of those you follow and see if their content makes you feel good or bad. If it makes you feel bad, unfollow them, and if you feel bad for unfollowing them, mute them so that their content doesn't fill up your feed. This way, you will be able to consume more positive content that will leave you in a better frame of mind.

The same goes with media content as we explored in Chapter 4, The Consumable Shitty Committee. If you are constantly watching the news or shows that are filled with negativity, such content is going to leave you feeling shit. Limit your time consuming these or, if you continue to engage with such media, focus more on positive content instead.

Taking these steps to remove the drains out of your physical and digital space will help clear the pathway to a more fulfilling life. There is likely to be some resistance that will prevent you from doing so, which is why, in the next chapter, The Pain In The (Secondary) Gain, we will explore what may be holding you back from living a more fulfilling life.

8

THE PAIN IN THE (SECONDARY) GAINS

"If you don't sacrifice for what you want, what you want becomes the sacrifice."
Proverb

Michael was born the fourth of seven children to his parents Katie and Sam and grew up in a 3-bedroom house on the outskirts of Manchester where, given there were nine people in his house, he never had any time or space for himself. In his family, Michael was closest to his younger brother who he often looked after as their dad was always out working and their mum was busy looking after the two youngest children. His older siblings commanded most of their dad's attention when he was at home due to their shared love of Football, leaving Michael absent of any real relationship with his mum or dad.

At school, Michael applied himself both to his school work and to sports, particularly rugby for which he had a natural talent, going on to catch the eye of the PE teacher who saw Michael's potential, harnessed it during lessons and encouraged Michael to sign up for the school rugby team. Whenever he would come home excited and proud of his performance on the rugby pitch, his mum would acknowledge his achievements by saying '*I'm so glad I don't have to worry about you.*' Though this was Michael's mum's way of expressing her love, it wasn't love in the form that Michael wanted; he wanted her attention to know that he mattered, that he was important. Whenever his dad came home, any achievement Michael had made on the rugby pitch that week wasn't celebrated or deemed important compared to one of his older siblings who were all playing football which, in their dad's eyes, was a real sport. He would often say to Michael '*When are you gonna give up that rugby nonsense and start playing a sport like football that can really earn you money?*'

Though he was not getting the love and attention he wanted from his parents, his sports teacher still believed in him and, at 14, Michael, who by this point had become a promising rugby player, was being scouted at a local school match by Manchester Rugby Club for their Under 15 team. The first half highlighted Michael's natural skill on the field but, in the second half when a player from the other side went in for a tackle, Michael's legs were taken out from under him and, as Michael fell to the ground, he heard something crack and was crippled in pain. Deemed to be more serious than just a sprain, Michael was rushed to the nearby hospital and his parents (both of whom weren't in attendance) were notified, with his mum quickly coming to be by his side as the doctors looked into it. Michael spent the next 12 hours in hospital, with his mum and dad taking it in turns to be with him. It turned out he had broken the bone in his left leg and would have to have a cast put on his leg to help his bones to heal.

Michael would be restricted in his ability to move around and would need to keep the cast on for at least six weeks before coming back to the hospital to do an X-ray to see how the bones were healing. During this time, Katie and Sam spent a lot of time looking after him and, at last, Michael finally no longer felt invisible to his parents. He finally felt seen by them and was able to get the love and attention he so desperately wanted and needed that was missing throughout his childhood. This attention created a story in Michael's head that the only way to get his needs met by his parents was by being ill. Six weeks later when back at the hospital to get the X-ray done, Michael had made real progress with his leg and the bone had almost healed, with the doctor telling him to come back in one week when they would be able to take the cast off.

Michael dreaded the thought of this, as once the cast was off, he would no longer be ill in the eyes of his parents and therefore he believed things would revert to the way they were before, where he would no longer get the attention he wanted or needed regardless of his school or rugby achievements. Over the next 18 months until Michael left secondary school, he would often fall ill and intentionally cause harm to himself on the rugby pitch, so as to get the love and attention from his parents. Though he was known for his strength of force as a scrum half, Michael was regularly dislocating one of his shoulders and once, during a school league final match when going in full force for a tackle on the rugby field, Michael ended up breaking the same leg he had broken the previous year. This second injury to the same leg resulted in the doctors informing Michael that this injury would end his chances of ever having a professional career as a rugby player. Whilst he was saddened by the news, Michael was getting what he had ultimately wanted all along which was the attention and love from his parents that he so desperately craved growing up.

This story is just one of many examples of clients that I have worked with over the years who have sabotaged their full potential in life. Often, it's not until they work through what is going on for them in a therapeutic or coaching capacity that they become consciously aware of how or why they are sabotaging themselves. In Michael's instance, he was partially aware of what was going on but didn't fully realise the sacrifices he would be making to his future by injuring himself at the time.

In section three of this book, I will be sharing more stories, highlighting the lessons learnt, and giving tools and techniques to help you master The Shitty Committee so that you can live a more fulfilling life. But no matter what I say in this book, it's Lori

Deschene who says it best, '*No one changes unless they want to. Not if you shame them, not if you use reason, emotion or tough love. There's only one thing that makes someone change: their own realisation that they need to do it. And there's only one time it will happen: when they decide they are ready.*'

By picking up this book, I can tell that you are ready to embark on this journey of change and, in many ways, you may have already taken steps to help you stop feeling like shit and move forward to start living a more fulfilling life. Perhaps at some point along that pathway, you have got stuck and want to get unstuck so you can continue moving forward. To help you look at and uncover what may be holding you back from making that change, I want to use a technique called Cartesian Logic to ask you four questions that will help you to see what may be holding you back and what, if any, secondary gains there are that keep you staying where you are.

Cartesian Logic works by asking you the four questions outlined in the diagram below, focusing on an area of your life in which you want to make a change. By answering each of the questions, it helps open up a different part of your brain and make you think about what you may gain or lose by making a specific change in your life. To help you understand it more, I'll fill in the below with an example of Cyndie, who wants to set up her own business after working with the same company for 15 years.

WHAT WOULD HAPPEN IF I DID?	WHAT WOULDN'T HAPPEN IF I DID?
I'd have the business I've always dreamed of I would be able to set my own schedule I'd get to work on things I want to work on I'd lose the company pension I currently have	I wouldn't have to work in the same office I wouldn't have to work normal office hours I wouldn't have financial security I wouldn't know how much money I'd make
WHAT WOULD HAPPEN IF I DIDN'T?	**WHAT WOULDN'T HAPPEN IF I DIDN'T?**
I'd stay in the same job I've been in for 15 years I'd always wonder 'What If?' I'd never get to see the looks of my family's faces when I opened my business I'd still have a regular income	I wouldn't die I wouldn't lose my current job I wouldn't run out of money

These responses are just a few of the answers that Cyndie gave and, as you can see by looking at some of her answers, whilst there are quite a few positives driving her towards change, for Cyndie, the pain of not living a more fulfilling life by staying in the same job for fifteen years, wasn't painful enough to overcome the secondary gain she got from a regular income, to start her new business.

Before we look at challenging any secondary gains you may have that are stopping you from achieving your full potential, I want you to look at the area/s of your life you want to change and write it down below:

____

____

From there I want you to go through the four questions below like the example we just went through and explore what comes up for you if you were to make that change. You can start in any section and work your way through each quadrant at your own pace. (Further help with this exercise can be found on the next page, and if you need more space to answer the questions, use Index 2).

WHAT WOULD HAPPEN IF I DID?	WHAT WOULDN'T HAPPEN IF I DID?
WHAT WOULD HAPPEN IF I DIDN'T?	**WHAT WOULDN'T HAPPEN IF I DIDN'T?**

If you get stuck with any more answers to the question in a quadrant, ask yourself "*and what else….*" followed by the question in the quadrant you are stuck in. A lot of people struggle with the '*what wouldn't happen if you didn't make that change?*', because it's a double negative, so if you get stuck , look at the answers Cyndie gave as a starting point and build on your answers from there.

Hopefully for most of you reading this, it has helped you become even clearer on why you should make that change in your life to fulfil your full potential, but I am sure for many of you reading this, it may have uncovered one or more secondary gains that are preventing you from taking action to fulfil your full potential and live the life you've always dreamed of.

To help look at those secondary gains a little bit more, I want you to do another exercise which is called the Seven Levels Deep exercise to help you get a deeper understanding of why that secondary gain is so important to you. The purpose of this exercise is to get out of your head and down into your heart, and whilst the questions continue to repeat themselves time and time again, every time you answer the question a newer deeper answer will unfold. We will then look at that underlying fear to take away the power of that secondary gain and turn it into fuel to help get you unstuck and propel you forward.

If you identified a secondary gain, I want you to write it down below

Now the next step is to look at why this secondary gain is so important to you by going 7 levels deep and asking the following seven questions.

Level 1 - What about your secondary gain is important to you?

Level 2 - Why is that important to you?

Level 3 - Why is that important to you?

Level 4 - And why is that important to you?

Level 5 - Why is that important to you?

Level 6 - Specifically why is that important to you?

Level 7 - And why is that important to you?

As I worked through this exercise with Cyndie, she started by saying '*I want to know I have enough money to cover all my expenses.*' As we continued through each level, she started to share that it was important to her because she didn't want to have to sacrifice certain things in her life. As we reached Level 6 Cyndie said, '*I don't want to go back to when I was a child where we didn't have any money and had to live out of my parents' car for six months*'. As the tears rolled down Cyndie's face I could see that it had awakened something within her, yet I knew there was still something else behind that answer (hence this exercise being called 7 Levels deep) and so when I asked her why it was important for her never to go backwards, she said because she wanted to be in control of her future, as she didn't have control of that situation growing up.

As Cyndie went through this process, she discovered that her relationship with money was much deeper than just paying her expenses. It was all about not going back to a time when she was homeless and wanting to be in control. However, with my help, Cyndie was able to reframe that situation and use that fear as fuel, and that's what we want you to do now. When you go through the 7 Levels Deep exercise and get to the seventh level to understand why that secondary gain is important to you and is keeping you stuck, I want you to take that limiting belief that The Shitty Committee is telling you and flip it on its head to use it as fuel to take massive action and go on to live a more fulfilling life and live to your full potential.

If we look at Cyndie again and her wanting to be in control of her life, every day Cyndie wasn't taking a step towards creating her new business she wasn't staying stuck, she was actually taking a step backwards further away from her dream. Every time she wasn't working on her new business and claiming control of her future career, she was letting the job she was currently in control her career, and we now live in a day and age where hardly anyone has a job for life, so whilst Cyndie wanted that security of a regular pay check it was never 100% guaranteed.

Cyndie wasn't ready to hand in her notice, up and leave to set up her new business straight away, but she was committed to prioritising her new business in her life outside of her job at the time, to build up her business in parallel with her job. Over the next six months, Cyndie committed daily to setting up her business, hiring her weaknesses to get things like her website designed, or finding manufacturers who could create the products her new business would sell and then, when the timing was right, she launched her own jewellery business. A year on from launching that business, sales continued to pick up online as she marketed and promoted her jewellery; and as the world started to open up again after the rolling lockdowns of the pandemic, Cyndie found herself renting stools at various markets not only in London but around the UK, to sell her jewellery, all whilst retaining her secure job.

Cyndie has already negotiated with her workplace to drop down from five to four days per week as her business continues to grow, and her goal is to work down to two days over the next six to 12 months with the aim of running her jewellery business full time in 18 months' time.

Now your seventh level deep of your secondary gain may also be like Cyndie's where you want to be in control, but it is highly likely that you also have a different answer. Here are two examples I hear regularly and two great counter arguments that can add fuel to propel you forward towards living a more fulfilling life and reaching your true potential.

Seventh Level Deep Response

I Don't Want To Be Alone

Counter Response To Propel You Forward

I Will Not Put Myself In Any Situations That Make Me Feel Alone.

As the late great Robin Williams said '*I used to think the worst thing in life was to end up alone. It's not. The worst thing in life is ending up with people who make you feel alone.*'

Seventh Level Deep Response
I Don't Want To Be A Failure
Counter Response To Propel You Forward
I Will Not Look At Anything As A Failure But Instead As Feedback I Can Grow And Learn From.

There's no guarantee of success but, as Wayne Gretzky said, *'You miss 100% of the shots you don't take.'* What will your counter response be to your Seven Levels Deep response?

Seven Levels Deep Response

____

____

Counter Response To Propel You Forward

____

____

If we are willing to look deeply enough within ourselves, there is always going to be a secondary gain that The Shitty Committee can cling on to and weaponize. It wants to keep you stuck and living in your comfort zone, rather than allowing you to step outside past the fear zone and into the learning and growth zone, so that you can start living a more fulfilling life.

The secret is not to avoid the root cause of the secondary gain because that will give The Shitty Committee what it needs to control you. Instead, uncover it by going seven levels deep, shining a spotlight on the root cause to expose it for what it is and turn that fear into fuel by reframing it to propel you forward, using your counter response any time the seven levels deep fear shows up. That way, you take a stride towards removing the power that The Shitty Committee has over you from making that change you deserve to make in your life.

Uncovering, exposing and removing the secondary gain is unlikely to be enough to help you break free from The Shitty Committee's control, so in the next chapter we are going to look at how to weather the storms that life brings your way before focusing in Section 3 on a whole host of ways you can master The Shitty Committee so you can live a more fulfilling life.

9

WEATHERING THE STORM

"Not all storms come to disrupt your life, some come to clear your path."
– An enlightened storm watcher

On a Sunday evening at the start of March 2020, I was at home packing my bags getting ready to embark on a two-week UK and Ireland tour to deliver the LIVELIVE initiative at Lewis Capaldi's shows. I turned on the news to see that Covid-19 was starting to become a more serious issue outside of China, with cases rising exponentially and concerns that it could be worse than both SARs and H1N1 (Swine Flu) that had occurred in the first decade of the new millennium.

Unaware of the scale of what would soon unravel around the world, we set out on the tour where each day the news would become more and more concerning about the impact of Coronavirus. Questions continued to arise on show days as to whether that show, and the remainder of the tour, would go ahead. Enquiries were coming through to us via email with at least 100 a day, and only increasing as the tour went on. Towards the tail end of the tour, you could feel the storm really ramping up, like a hurricane when its winds strengthen from a tropical storm up the categories. By the time we were leaving Ireland after the two Dublin shows, we could feel the pandemic really taking a grip, as Ireland went into lockdown, mere hours after we left. As we arrived in London for the Wembley shows, both the support acts (who were American) had flown back to the US due to the US Government imposing a travel ban on all European countries.

Even though we were all aware to an extent of what was unfolding, when you are on tour you often live very much in a bubble where it's tour bus, hotel, venue and repeat day in day out, with little to no connection to the real world. But by the night of the second Wembley show, the seriousness of the pandemic was now starting to sink in for everyone, as there was an eeriness in the air, brought on by the departure of the US support acts, many businesses in the UK telling their employees they were to work from home the following week and the seriousness of how the pandemic was shaping up abroad with cases exploding in Europe - especially Italy, which had overtaken China as the new epicentre. As we reached Aberdeen for the final date of the tour, none of us could have foreseen what would happen not only to the live industry but the whole world and, as we said our goodbyes to the crew that night, it would turn out to be the last live full-capacity concert for almost 18 months.

Whilst people like Bill Gates and organisations such as WHO (World Health Organisation) and the CDC (Center for Disease Control and Prevention) were often talking about the threat of a global pandemic over the years, most of us never even thought about pandemics or the impact a virus could have on our daily lives, and as Covid-19 really started to ramp up, I don't think anyone knew how long-lasting and devastating the pandemic would be. Some businesses and business sectors were able to easily make the transition from working in offices to working remotely at home through the use of their digital devices and Zoom but, for some sectors like the live performance sector or the wider service sector, those industries were devastated by the ongoing impacts of the pandemic.

. . .

The pandemic is a great recent example of how the world has collectively weathered the storm; not one person has been unaffected in some way, shape or form from the impacts of Covid-19. That said, we've also all experienced it very differently. You will have likely heard the expression, '*We're all in the same boat!*' Well, I call bullshit on that. We're not all in the same boat, but we are often all in the same storm, as the Covid-19 pandemic has highlighted to us. Some of us are blissfully unaware on a cruise ship, some of us are living our best lives on a yacht, unaffected or potentially even thriving in the storm. Some of us are in a rowboat trying to navigate the choppy waters and preventing the boat from capsizing. And some of us, like Jack and Rose in Titanic, are clinging to the plank of wood for dear life.

You see, at any one moment in life, we could all be in any of these locations depending on the storm that comes our way, be that job loss, divorce, bereavement, or another challenge. We could be on the cruise ship, the yacht, the rowboat, or we could be on the plank of wood. Yet no matter which location you find yourself in, you can still be impacted by the storm. William Arthur Ward, a great motivational writer of the twentieth century, also loved using boat analogies and he had a great way of framing the way we view things in life. For if we are in a boat in a storm, you'll find three types of people:

1. The **optimist** who expects the wind to change
2. The **pessimist** who complains about the wind and
3. The **realist** who adjusts the sails.

Whilst I don't know the individual situations that each of you are going through or have gone through in life, I know that the way we approach storms that come into our life will either fuel The Shitty Committee to run rife and keep us swept up in that storm, or look to find a way out of it so that we can survive or even thrive. As the late great Viktor Frankl once wrote in his book, '*Man's Search For Meaning*', about his time in a Nazi concentration camp during the Second World War, man can take everything away from you, but no one can take away from you the ability to choose one thought over the other. In this chapter, what I want to focus on is how to navigate a storm, to find and forge a path forward through it to calmer waters where it's clear sailing from there.

Expanding on the story at the start of this chapter, during those first few weeks in the pandemic, one of my business partners Ric Salmon (with whom I founded a charity called Point One Project alongside Movember founder JC and artist Ryan Keen) and his management company was devastated by the pandemic and the loss of the live sector, which took away a significant portion of their revenues. However, rather than being in a pessimistic frame of mind where he could be defeated by the pandemic, he chose to be a realist, who realised that he would need to find other ways to create an income stream. He went on to create Driift, a company that would produce and promote immersive and interactive online live ticketed events.

This not only created a new revenue stream for Ric and those with whom he partnered to form Driift, but also gave artists an opportunity to perform again in a variety of different settings and venues including The Royal Albert Hall, The Natural History Museum and countless others; rather than live streaming through their social media platforms from their homes to a digital audience, he created a service that upped the production value, enabling the artists to monetise their performances and allowing them and their crew and band to earn money from performing live again. These shows by a variety of different artists including Niall Horan, Kylie Minogue and Andrea Bocelli, whilst not replacing the live concert experience, allowed fans to still see many of their favourite artists perform in a full show in a live setting from the comfort of their own home and, as live shows have now returned, this format can complement and enhance the live experience.

Ric's ability to weather the storm of the pandemic by creating

Driift, has also helped him navigate other storms for Driift to overcome, which in the past have included the way songwriters get paid for live streamed shows or the unfortunate technical incident on the Glastonbury live stream when a percentage of customers couldn't get in for part of the stream. Like Ric's experience through the pandemic, and the hurricane season in the Atlantic Ocean, in life there will be several storms that arise each and every year. Some people may miss every storm, as the storms don't come across their path; some may only come across one storm that has little to no impact; some may come across a number of storms in succession; and some may come across one devastating storm that leaves them picking up the pieces afterwards. But it's worth remembering that:

Not all storms come to disrupt your life, some come to clear your path.

I want you to think about a storm that you either faced in the past or are currently facing and just view it through the lens of the three different options that William Arthur Ward shared. Write down each perspective you have on the situation.

The Optimist

____

____

____

The Pessimist

____

____

____

The Realist

____

____

____

When looking through the pessimist lens, Martin Seligman, founder of Positive Psychology, said the pessimist looks at things through the three Ps:

1. **Pervasive** – that this current situation impacting one area will impact or reflect on all areas of your life
2. **Permanent** – that this current situation will go on forever
3. **Personal** – that this current situation is personal

Let's look at an example. Sarah is a 35-year-old branch manager at NatWest who has worked for the same bank for 10 years. She has worked her way up from cashier to branch manager and has been in the same position for the past 3 years. One day, Sarah sees a new job posted on the company intranet for a role at head office and feels like this is the next logical career step for her. She has reached a ceiling in her current role and so she decides to put herself forward for the position. After several rounds of interviews, Sarah makes it to the final stage where three individuals are up for the role. Over a week passes after the final round of interviews and, as the wait to find out becomes unbearable for Sarah, she reaches out to HR via email, to get an update, where she is informed that an external candidate was the successful applicant. Hearing the news, Sarah is devastated and stays in this mindset for several weeks, impacting her work at the branch and having others complain about her. For Sarah has chosen to continue to look at things through a pessimistic light with The Shitty Committee reaffirming those thoughts saying, '*I'm going to be a branch manager forever*' (permanent), '*I am not good at anything in my life*' (pervasive) and 'I *didn't get the job because they don't like me*' (personal).

. . .

If Sarah were to shift perspectives and look at it through the realist or optimist lens, realists and optimists see storms in their life as an STI which is:

1. **Specific** – this situation is only focused on a certain area of my life and isn't a reflection on other areas
2. **Temporary** – this situation will pass
3. **Impersonal** – this isn't about me

If we were to go back to the example of Sarah not getting the job and she was to switch from a pessimistic view to an optimistic or realistic view, Sarah would be able to counter The Shitty Committee with '*I didn't get the job this time* (temporary) *but that doesn't mean I'm a failure* (specific). *If I get feedback on what I can do to improve my chances the next time there is a new role and work towards building on those skills or qualities, I will be more likely to be successful in securing that promotion.*' (impersonal)

If you were to reflect on the three different perspectives that you previously wrote down in this chapter, which of the three perspectives speak the most to you? I'm guessing most of you have chosen the realist. I'm also sure also that some of you reading this picked out the optimistic mindset, with the view that thinking optimistically or all those positive mantras and affirmations you tell yourself each day are all you need for the universe to give you what you want. You may often see titles of books like '*Ask and It Is Given*' by Ester and Jerry Hicks, or '*Think and Grow Rich*' by Napoleon Hill and believe that all you need to do is ask or think your way to a more fulfilling life, but unless you get past the cover and dive deep into the content of these books and take uncomfortable action to work towards resolving those issues or to working towards those goals, all the positive thinking in the world on its own is not going to get you to that destination. You need to take action.

I'm sure you've heard the expression '*Good things come to those who wait*' and, to an extent, that's true. For in life, we often work on something, get to a certain point and then wait for the results to occur. But as I've grown older, I've come to realise that this quote wasn't fully formed and was often a limiting belief put on us as children to keep us in line. It allows The Shitty Committee to keep us in our comfort zone, not moving towards a more fulfilling life at a pace befitting of our abilities. So, I'd like to update and reframe that quote in a different light to see how it sits with you:

Good things come to those who wait... but GREAT things come to those who don't.

I want you to either go back and look at that example you used earlier of a storm you are currently experiencing or have experienced in the past. Or, if you prefer, you can also think of a new one. Using the STI outlook, note down the answers to the following questions:

Specific - In which area(s) does this storm impact my life? And does it stop me from doing everything in every area of my life?

____

____

____

Temporary - How long will this storm realistically go on for if I zoom out from being in the storm to see it from above like a satellite over earth?

____

____

____

Impersonal - Is this storm really about me, or is it about things beyond my control, about other people's issues and not my own?

____

____

____

Once you allow yourself to become clear on the storm that you are facing in your life, you prevent The Shitty Committee from taking a hold and you can start to identify what to do to weather the storm.

So, do you want something good out of your life? Or do you want something great? I don't know about you, but the fact you're reading this book tells me that good has only got you so far in life but great is where you want to be.

In Section 2 of this book, we have taken the time to understand when The Shitty Committee makes you its slave. From the ways it shows up to the ways other people you surround yourself with make you feel. From evaluating and evolving the company you keep to the secondary gains you get from staying stuck and how changing your outlook can help you weather the storm. It's now time to move onto Section 3, where you will be guided through a variety of different ways to master The Shitty Committee, so you can start (or continue) living a more fulfilling life.

SECTION 3

HOW TO MASTER THE SHITTY COMMITTEE TO LIVE A MORE FULFILLING LIFE

10

THAT'S THE SPIRIT

"Being spiritual doesn't always mean that you are positive. Get the fuck out my face whilst I balance my energies." – An Unknown Badass Woman

Thomas Edison is one of the most famous inventors of all time and, throughout his life in the 19th and 20th centuries, he accumulated over 1,093 patents in the United States alone and over 512 patents worldwide for a plethora of different designs and inventions. Many of these formed the foundations of things we continue to use and rely on today, including:

- The Phonograph (enabling us to listen to music)
- The Kinetoscope (enabling us to watch moving images)
- The Electric Lamp
- The Light Bulb (the incandescent light bulb)
- The Carbon Microphone (which greatly improved the telephone)

In many cases, Edison's inventions weren't original, but improvements on earlier inventions by others which he enhanced in various ways, shapes or forms to elevate the products to new levels and mass appeal. Edison was an extremely intelligent individual, like many of his peers at the time who were focused on inventing, designing and modifying products. But it wasn't his intellect alone that led Edison to become one of the greatest inventors of all time. It was his mindset. He had a different way of approaching his work which helped him to excel whilst others fell by the wayside. A curious reporter once asked Edison about the perceived 'failures' in his research and construction of the electric lightbulb. Edison's response offers an insight into his approach:

'I have not failed; I've just found 10,000 ways that don't work!'

For Edison, every time he didn't invent the electric lightbulb, he became one step closer to inventing it. For every attempt he made at inventing the lightbulb that didn't work, he had one fewer pathway to explore until he reached the right pathway that would take him to his destination. Many other inventors were also pursuing the invention of the incandescent lightbulb but they, one by one, let their repeated attempts knock their confidence and enthusiasm; Edison didn't waiver, he continued to move forward. He refused to let his spirit be dampened or diminished and it was with that mindset and attitude that he paved the way to become one of the greatest inventors of all time.

There are millions of other examples of individuals who have used more than just their intelligence throughout history to fulfil their full potential. You only have to look at the educational system in the Western World today to see that the focus remains on measuring an individual's IQ through assignments and exams, when instead I believe we should be focusing on building people's EQ (emotional intelligence) and SQ (spiritual intelligence) to fulfil their full potential, to equip them with the ability to not let The Shitty Committee take over when up against a perceived setback.

. . .

Some of you reading this will have heard the term EQ used in the last 20 years, whilst most (including myself, until relatively recently) won't have heard of SQ, and so I've explained IQ, EQ and SQ in more detail below.

IQ

IQ is an intelligence quotient that provides a score based on a set of standardised tests or subtests designed to assess human intelligence. The scores are broken down into different bands that denote where your intellect lies compared to the national average.

Low = 1-70
Below Average = 71-84
Average = 85 – 115
Above Average = 116 – 144
High = 145 – 159
Genius = 160+

EQ

EQ is emotional intelligence (otherwise known as emotional quotient) that highlights the ability of an individual to understand, use and manage their own emotions in positive ways to relieve stress, communicate effectively, empathise with others, overcome challenges and diffuse conflict.

SQ

SQ is spiritual quotient, a term coined by Danah Zohar in 1997 that helps to indicate spiritual parallels with IQ, where spiritual is distinct from religiosity. Zohar outlined 12 principles that underline SQ. These include:

1. self-awareness
2. spontaneity

3. being vision and value-led
4. having compassion
5. celebrating diversity
6. fielding independence
7. having humility
8. asking fundamental why questions
9. ability to reframe
10. positive use of adversity
11. a sense of vocation and
12. having holism, aka a sense of belonging.

When looking at these three quotients, I feel that SQ is the most important quotient we should be focusing on teaching individuals, followed by EQ and then IQ. For having an unwavering spirit can see you not only through the best of times but the hardest of times too. Developing your emotional quotient can help you to navigate your emotions when storms enter your pathway and manage the impact of other people's emotions on you. For me, IQ comes last, as I believe everyone to be equally intelligent, just in different areas.

I know some of you may question the last statement but let me share an example to illustrate that point. Imagine you have travelled abroad with some friends for a holiday and, after dinner one night, you stop off at a bar where they happen to be hosting a quiz. Invited in by the bar owner, you all think you are smart individuals with high IQs who usually perform well in quizzes and so you enter and sign up. As the quiz gets going in the first two rounds, which are both general knowledge, your perspective holds true as your team get maximum points in each round, giving you a grand total of 20 points (10 per round) and you lead the other eight teams who are also performing well but are around the 15-18 points mark.

As the next round comes up, the subject is on Aussie Rules football. Unbeknown to you, this is a popular bar for Australians and all the other teams that are playing in the quiz are from Australia. You and your teammates have no idea about the sport and, as such, fail to answer any of the questions correctly. Your team score stays at 20 after three rounds and the other teams, who all get 9 or 10 out of 10 in this round, move past you with 25-28 points. After three rounds, you have gone from first place to last in the quiz.

You see, intelligence or knowledge about a certain subject is often only relevant in the environment in which it is required and so, whilst being knowledgeable in the area you are working in can see you advance in your career, knowledge alone isn't the deciding factor in fulfilling your full potential. As Albert Einstein, once wisely shared:

'Everybody is a genius. But if you judge a fish by its ability to climb a tree, it will live its whole life believing that it is stupid.'

Let's look at another example of how your SQ can lead you to a more fulfilling life. Could you off the top of your head tell me who won Season 3 of American Idol? No, me neither, and I worked in the music industry for 20 years (it was an artist named Fantasia by the way). But if I were to ask you if you had heard of Jennifer Hudson, I'm pretty sure most of you will have heard of the Academy Award-winning actress who starred alongside Beyonce in Dreamgirls and was handpicked by Queen of Soul, Miss Aretha Franklin herself, to play her in the biopic of her life.

You see, Jennifer Hudson was also in Season 3 of American Idol, but ended up finishing seventh. She didn't allow that setback to knock her spirit. She continued to pursue her dreams of becoming a recording artist and an actress, and is well on her way to becoming part of an elite club of EGOT (Emmy, Grammy, Oscar and Tony) winners, having already bagged both an Oscar and Grammy. And she has achieved all of this in the face of devastating personal tragedy. Since being in the limelight, her mother, brother and nephew were all murdered by her brother-in-law; but she did not allow these devastating actions to knock her spirit. She soldiered on through the pain and adversity, believing in a higher power to guide her through.

There are many other examples, especially in reality show competitions, where the winner of the show isn't the one that goes on to have the breakout success following their win. For every Kelly Clarkson and Leona Lewis who win these talent shows, there are others like Steve Brookstein and Lee DeWyze who, after winning, shortly fade back into obscurity. When One Direction appeared on X Factor, they didn't win either (they didn't even come second, they came third), but whilst they were down, they were not out and they used their SQ, along with the team around them, to use that upset or setback to propel them forwards.

Whilst I was growing up, academic work provided me with comfort when I was being bullied or made to feel isolated by others in my school. Having no friends to spend time with, I put all my energy and effort into studying and became a straight A student, exceeding every teacher's expectations and leaving with the highest grades in my school year. However, whilst I gained a lot of intelligence (IQ), my EQ and SQ were very low and I would be often be held hostage by The Shitty Committee.

Through my own personal development journey in therapy, with mentors and coaches, and on my own training to become a coach, NLP practitioner, therapist and what I call '*A Transitionist*' (that is someone skilled at coping with or managing transitions in any field), I have built up both my EQ and SQ and realise now that I would much rather be a C student with a high EQ and SQ than an A student with a high IQ and low EQ and SQ. That's not to say that someone can't have all three at a high level, I'm simply saying that to overcome The Shitty Committee to live a more fulfilling live, the SQ has to come first, then the EQ and finally the IQ.

Using IQ as the main marker of intellect doesn't automatically define who is going to live the most fulfilling life or be the most successful. Many individuals with a high IQ have a natural talent when it comes to IQ-based tests and therefore find it easier to score in the upper echelons; those who have natural talent and don't have to work hard on things can often become complacent and not put in the skill required to continually push forward. Down the line, this may put them at a disadvantage whilst those who continually work hard on honing their skills go on to master that skill and propel past that naturally talented individual who didn't put the work in. This often happens in the sporting world, where a young child has an abundance of talent but doesn't harness and work on it, and soon gets overtaken by others on the team or in the sport they are in, leaving people questioning what happened to that talented individual.

That's why the expression '*winning isn't everything*' is so true; it's what you do with the platform that your win provides that defines the outcome. And for those who don't win, being the underdog has several advantages too.

Angela Duckworth; a professor of psychology, talks about this extensively in her work on *Grit*, where she has spent decades looking at what it is that determines the ability of one individual over another to succeed. As a result of Duckworth's extensive research in this area, she finds herself working with a large number of organisations and governments to help them determine the most suitable person for the job, which ninety-nine percent of the time isn't the one with the highest IQ but those with the most grit – or, as I'm calling it here, an unwavering SQ. Many individuals in life rely on their talent alone to help them to lead a more fulfilling life, but when an obstacle crosses their path, talent on its own is often shown not to be enough and The Shitty Committee has a field day telling those individuals to give up, to quit, or to stop pursuing something which feels unattainable. Then there are those who match their natural talent with skill, putting in hours of work to hone their craft. This can get you a lot further but Duckworth believes there is one key ingredient missing to help you live a more fulfilling life… effort.

As Duckworth notes in her book on Grit '*Without effort, your talent is nothing more than your unmet potential. Without effort, your skill is nothing more than what you could have done but didn't. With effort, talent becomes skill and, at the very same time, effort makes skills productive.*' There are many people with talent or skill that don't live a more fulfilling life and have spent vast amounts of their time singing or saying their '*shoulda, woulda, couldas*'; but those who combine their skill and talent with effort stand a greater chance of living a more fulfilling life and heading a lot further down the pathway, even if they are perceived by most as the underdog, the one who will never succeed.

One of the world's leading coaches, Dean Graziosi, speaks about this a lot in the work he does. He even wrote a book about it called '*The Underdog Advantage*' where he highlighted that being the underdog has several distinct advantages which include:

1. The underdog has nothing to lose and therefore is more willing to take risks
2. The underdog is able to use the power of the words '*you can't*' to their advantage
3. The underdog has the ability to act fast and move quickly
4. The underdog is relentlessly resourceful, utilising whatever they can to succeed
5. The underdog is thirsty in educating themselves to take them to the next level
6. The underdog doesn't have to care what others think, as all eyes aren't on them

When looking at this through the lens of your spiritual quotient (SQ), sometimes being the underdog actually strengthens your SQ if you are able to harness it correctly. For when you are the underdog, The Shitty Committee will come along with bells and whistles saying things like, '*you aren't as good as so and so*', '*you may as well give up now, you are never going to succeed*' and so on, using whatever evidence it can to keep you in that comfort zone, rather than letting you step outside into that fear zone, learning zone or growth zone. But as Woody Allen says '*Eighty percent of success in life is about showing up.*' So if you continue to show up despite what The Shitty Committee is saying to you and use it instead as fuel to motivate you, the percentages are in your favour that you are more than likely going to live a more fulfilling life.

In at least one area in our lives, we are seen as the underdog, whether that be by others or ourselves, and that is a beautiful gift that has been offered to us to strengthen our SQ. To strength your SQ, all you need are the following four Cs to see you through:

1. Confidence
2. Commitment
3. Courage and
4. Clarity

Let's go ahead and break down each one a little further to see how you can use the four Cs to strengthen your SQ to fulfil your full potential.

1. Confidence

Confidence in yourself is the first area you need to build when you are the underdog, to fulfil your full potential and use to your advantage. Confidence is having a clear state of mind that you have the ability to achieve whatever you set your mind to. Combined with the other three Cs, it will get you exactly where you need to go. But one thing you must remember is not to confuse confidence with arrogance or ignorance, for being confident is knowing you have or will acquire the abilities to achieve what you set your mind to; ignorance and arrogance get in the way of that, blurring your vision and leaving you open to blind spots that will hinder you on the pathway to achieving your full potential.

Think back to your childhood for a moment and the story about the race between the hare and the tortoise that perfectly illustrates this concept. The tortoise was seen by everyone as the underdog in the race, but she continued to believe that she could win the race; whereas the hare, aware of his speed compared to the tortoise, became overly confident and believed he already had the win in the bag before he even started. As the gun shot signalled the start of the race, the hare sped off into a decisive lead and, as he approached the finish line, realising all the time it would take for the tortoise to catch up, he decided to take a nap by the tree nearby. The tortoise, continuing at its own pace with one leg in front of the other never giving up and as she approached the finish line, realised that the hare hadn't yet crossed the finish line and that she was now in front. The hare, starting to awaken from his nap, realised the tortoise had not only caught up but had overtaken him and, though trying desperately to get across the line with his speed, his overconfidence in his abilities and complacency that led him to take a nap meant he wouldn't be able to close the gap ahead of the tortoise.

So what can you do or what can you utilise to build your confidence on the pathway to a more fulfilling life? And what can you do to ensure your confidence doesn't turn into arrogance or complacency?

____

____

____

____

If you are struggling with ideas or need help building your confidence, Chapter 14 – Where Are My M&M's? - has some great techniques to help you build it.

2. Commitment

To fulfil your full potential and overcome the obstacles that The Shitty Committee will put in your way, you need to be fully committed to achieving your full potential in whatever area you are working on. No-one is able to achieve their full potential by being half in half out; you need to go all in and commit 100% to what you've set your mind to.

For example, if you are only half committed to reaching and

sustaining your ideal weight, you are either going to not hit your ideal weight because you are not committing to regularly working out, eating the right foods and doing the things that you know will help you achieve your ideal weight or, once you get there, you won't stay committed to sustaining the practices that help you achieve your ideal weight. This will see you slide backwards, further and further away from your ideal weight and back to your starting point or potentially even further away from your ideal weight than when you started.

So how can you make a commitment to yourself today to ensure you continue on the pathway to a more fulfilling life? What steps do you need to take to make that commitment, be that shuffling your schedule around to set the time needed to commit or investing in x or y to help you get to where you want to go?

3. Courage

Brene Brown is one of the world's leading experts in the area of courage and a lot of her research as a professor, lecturer, and author has helped us to better understand what it means to be courageous. In Brown's infamous Ted Talk '*The Power Of Vulnerability*' (which is the fifth most viewed Ted Talk of all time), she highlights that we can't be courageous without first being vulnerable. Brown shares, '*Vulnerability is the courage to show up and be seen even when you can't control the outcome.*' Whether that's approaching a stranger in a bar that you find attractive, speaking up in a meeting to share an idea, or stepping into a new environment, having courage requires you to be vulnerable, and that's one of the last things The Shitty Committee wants to you to do, because there are so many possible negative or worst-case scenarios it can conjure up. Being courageous is really all about being vulnerable, ignoring all those negative or worst-cast scenarios The Shitty Committee espouses and leaning into whatever it is that is holding you back from living a more fulfilling life.

For my 37th birthday, I decided to tick off one of the scariest of the 200 items on my Fuck-It List (my own take on a bucket list); sky diving. I have always been petrified of heights; my fear has stopped me going up the Eiffel Tower, going on certain rides at theme parks and, once having psyched myself up to go to the top of the Empire State Building when walking outside around the top, I nearly crushed the bones in my poor friend Michelle's hand and clung to the wall - that's how scared I was. Over the years I have learned – or was forced to learn - to face my fear of heights; for several months, I worked on the top floor of the tallest building west of Chicago (the US bank that gets blown up in the movie, Independence Day). But that day, sky diving out of a plane, the fear was well and truly back, and if I was going to jump, I needed to be courageous when exiting the plane. It's obviously not natural for anyone to jump out of a moving vehicle 15,000 feet above the ground, and so I kept repeating the mantra (which we'll discuss more in Chapter 14) '*Everything you want in life is on the other side of fear itself.*' As the door was opened, I edged towards it and, before I knew it, I was out of the plane and free falling before the parachute kicked in, enjoying one of the best experiences of my life.

For me, living a more fulfilling life is all about stepping outside my comfort zone and doing things I wouldn't normally do, like sky diving or writing a book. For you, it may be reaching your ideal weight or starting and running a successful business. Whatever it is, it takes courage and vulnerability to step outside the comfort zone The Shitty Committee wants to keep you in, so that you can grow and lead that more fulfilling life.

What courageous steps do you need to take to step outside your comfort zone to live a more fulfilling life? List all of them, no matter how big or small, so that you can become clear or what steps or hurdles The Shitty Committee may use to hold you back:

4. Clarity

The last C you need to strengthen your SQ to start living a more fulfilling life is clarity. Clarity is so important, for if you don't have clarity on where you are heading, you are more than likely going to head in the wrong direction. Sure, on the pathway to living a more fulfilling life, there may be diversions that take you on a different route or potholes in the road that leave you stuck or needing to change a tyre, but like a GPS device, unless you know where you are going to and where you are starting from, it can't calculate the route for you or help provide alternative routes if the main route is no longer viable. You need to get very clear on where you are going, how you are going to get there, what you will need along the way and why you are heading there in the first place. Once you become clear on this, add in the courage, commitment and confidence you have collected and you can become an unstoppable force towards fulfilling your potential that The Shitty Committee has no chance of stopping.

How can you become crystal clear about your destination of living a more fulfilling life? I want you to have 20-20 vision on exactly what that looks like (e.g. being 28 lbs lighter in a red bikini on my holiday in 6 months time, or making £150,000 a year in net-profit in my business by the 3rd year in operation). We will cover the steps you need to take to get there in the next chapter, so for now just focus on being really clear on exactly what you want, the more specific the better.

Now you have the answers to the 4 Cs that can strengthen your SQ, I want you to regularly check in and refer back to them. I would recommend at least once a month, if not more, and adjust them accordingly if need be to ensure you continue to stay on track towards that pathway to a more fulfilling life. This will help in keeping The Shitty Committee at bay, preventing it from diminishing your spirit and keeping you trapped from living a more fulfilling live.

In closing this chapter, remember this: whilst IQ is important, having all the knowledge in the world isn't going to result in you living that more fulfilling life. You need to take uncomfortable action and, to do that, you need to be able to strengthen both your EQ - so that you can handle the emotional impacts of setbacks as they come along - and your SQ - so that nothing knocks your spirit on your way to achieving your full potential.

Before we move on to the next chapter on how to 'Slay In Your Lane', I'll leave you with these parting words from the former UK Prime Minister, Sir Winston Churchill, who once said '*Success consists of going from failure to failure without loss of enthusiasm.*' Another great quote from him to remember as you work to strengthen your SQ is, '*Success is not final, failure is not fatal, it is the courage to continue that counts.*'

11

SLAY IN YOUR LANE

"Your time is limited, so don't waste it living someone else's life." – Steve Jobs

Slay = *To kill it, be successful in, elevate in an area (or areas) of your life.*

It was 20th October 1968 on a warm autumn evening in Mexico City at the Olympics when the world of athletics and, more specifically, the high jump was about to change forever. For an unknown high jumper called Dick Fosbury from Portland, USA, was about to do something that had never been done before.

The high jump had been a staple event at the Olympics ever since the modern Olympic Games started in 1896 and, as with any event, as the years had passed, techniques had been tweaked and enhanced, leading to records being broken and new standards being set for emerging athletes to compete in the field. When the high jump started, athletes would attempt their jumps originally by jumping from a standing start; and, as the years passed, the styles evolved to include a scissor jump, a western roll and a straddle. The straddle jump became the 'go to' jump in the sport, with Fosbury's hero, Valery Brumel of the Soviet Union (as it was then known), winning the 1964 Olympic Games, breaking world record after world record as he continued to elevate the high jump to new heights.

Fosbury, by his own admission, was a lousy straddler, often failing to meet the 5ft (1.5m) height requirement to jump at many high school meets and knew he would never be able to reach the heights of his hero's success due to his poor technique. At this point, Fosbury could have given up his pursuit to be a high jumper, but instead he married his engineering know-how with his natural technique as he ran up to the bar. By applying some mechanics, Fosbury learnt that by arching his back, his centre of gravity could stay below the bar, even as his body sailed over it, giving him the ability to soar over the bar at heights he was previously unable to achieve from the straddle technique. Equipped with this knowledge, Fosbury continued to hone his talent, honouring the way he both approached the bar as he ran up to it and the mechanical statistics that backed up his evidence, allowing him to continue to make progressive strides towards the heights that his hero Brumel was jumping.

At 21 years old, as the autumn night set in at the Estadio Olympico Universitario, Fosbury was clearing height after height with his unique technique on his first attempt and, as the bar rose over 2 metres and continued to rise up each round, he started to see his competitors fall by the wayside, until 2 metres 22 centimetres with only three competitors left. Fosbury once again cleared the height at his first attempt, equalling the Olympic record set by his hero Brumel, with his US teammate Ed Caruthers managing to sail across the height on his second attempt, leaving a two-way race after Valentin Gavrilov of the Soviet Union failed to clear the height on all three attempts. As the bar was raised to 2.24m, Fosbury missed the bar on his first attempt and by, the second attempt both he and his US teammate, Caruthers, had also missed it.

However, Fosbury's skills were just as much in his head as in his legs and he psyched himself up for each jump, getting the crowd on his side and getting them to will him over the bar. With his third attempt, he managed to clear the height, and his leap over the bar at 2.24 metres set a new Olympic Record and won him a gold medal. Since those Olympics, high jumpers all over the world have taken on the technique that Fosbury created and where, once upon a time, he was the only athlete jumping in this style, as I write this now following the 2021 Olympics Games, every high jumper jumps in the style now known as the '*Fosbury Flop*'.

You may be asking yourself why I am sharing this story of an athlete from over half a century ago. I'm doing so because it perfectly encapsulates the title of this chapter, Slay In Your Lane. When Fosbury came to the realisation that he couldn't jump the way his idol Brumel did, he didn't stay focused on his inability to compete with Brumel or try and improve his straddle technique that frequently failed to get him clear of the 5ft height requirement to enter high school meets around the state of Oregon. Instead, he looked at the abilities he did possess, using not only the data that he could see within himself as he approached the bar to jump over and clear it, but he also tapped into his mechanical knowledge to explore how his abilities could help him clear the heights he felt unachievable using the go to technique in the mid-1960s.

Fosbury's commitment to harnessing his knowledge, his abilities and his strengths, rather than focusing on his weaknesses or comparing himself to others who were doing better than him with a technique that didn't tap into his full potential, allowed Fosbury to step outside of the comfort zone. Instead of following the path of those before him in the sport, he forged a new pathway that not only harnessed his strengths, but elevated the high jump to a whole new level.

Let me give you another example by fast-forwarding a couple of decades to the 1980s. In late 1981, a Danish drummer by the name of Lars Ulrich placed an advert in a Los Angeles newspaper which read '*drummer looking for other metal musicians to jam with Tygers of Pan Tang, Diamond Head and Iron Maiden.*' Two guitarists responded to the advert including James Hetfield. Although Ulrich didn't at that point form the band, he reached out to Metal Blade Records founder, Brian Slagel, to ask if he could record a song for the label's upcoming compilation album, Metal Massacre. With Slagel accepting, Ulrich recruited Hetfield to sing and play rhythm guitar with Ulrich on drums, which led to Metallica officially forming on 28th October 1981.

Wanting to expand the group, Metallica placed another advertisement in the press looking for a lead guitarist in early 1982. When Dave Mustaine responded and met Hetfield and Ulrich, the two were impressed with Mustaine's expensive guitar equipment and ability and invited him to join Metallica. However, their union was to be a short one when, a little over a year after Mustaine joined, he was fired from the group with the band citing his alcohol and drug abuse along with his violent outbursts being the reasons for his departure.

Mustaine, pissed at being kicked out from the band before Metallica's debut album was released, left him furious and he vowed to become bigger and more successful than Metallica. He formed his own band Megadeth. I won't bore you with the ins and outs of their respective journeys, but Megadeath went on to sell tens of millions of albums over the subsequent three decades and build their career up from nothing to perform at arenas around the world, becoming known as one of the big four of American thrash metal along with Anthrax, Slayer and Metallica. I'm sure you can all agree they are pretty successful, but Dave Mustaine didn't think or feel so. He was constantly caught in what is known as Musterbation, a term coined by the renowned father of CBT (Cognitive Behavioural Therapy), Albert Ellis, that leads people to distort the way they think and live their lives owing to a set of rules or demands that are often excessive, impractical and unhealthy. Mustaine would often utter things like '*I must be better than Metallica*', 'I *must sell more records that Metallica*', and '*I must perform at bigger venues than Metallica*'; his metric of success was not based on comparing himself to his own achievements of previous sales or tours but to the achievements of someone else, in this case his former bandmates in Metallica.

Metallica went on to sell four times as many records as

Megadeth with over 130 million sales worldwide, and they continue to perform in stadiums around the world 30 years on from forming. Unlike Mustaine, Hetfield and Ulrich weren't focused on how they must be better than Megadeth but focused instead on whether they could be better than they were yesterday, if they could improve their shows, their records, their playing abilities. A lot of Mustaine's energy was spent focusing on competing with Metallica, when the only competition we truly have in life is with ourselves.

Don't get me wrong, I know in many fields or business sectors, competition runs rife, and that there can be only one winner of the 100m Olympic final, one winner of the World Cup, or one person at No.1 on the Official Singles or Album Charts; but if you focus your energy on what your perceived competitors are doing, you take away vital energy that could be utilised on improving your own abilities or your team's abilities. Think of the following examples: the individuals who won the 100m Olympic final (Usain Bolt and Elaine Thompson-Herah) in 2016 aren't necessarily going to be the winners in 2024. The winners of the World Cup in 2018 (France) didn't even make it through to the knockout stages of the competition in 2010. If you are an artist and you determine your success by chart positions, your perceived competitors on the charts in December are Mariah Carey, Wham, Michael Bublé and a whole host of other Christmas songs that flood the charts in the run up to Christmas. However, come January, all of those tracks and nearly every artist with the exception of Ariana Grande and Justin Bieber who have their own modern Christmas classics are nowhere to be seen; and therefore no longer your perceived competition until December rolls round again.

You see, sometimes your perceived competition is ahead of you, and sometimes they are behind you, but if you attach your success to the achievements of others, The Shitty Committee is going to run wild, coming at you any time that your perceived competition may be doing better than you. It will tell you that '*you are a failure*', '*you aren't good enough*', '*you should quit*' and a myriad of other vitriol. It is therefore so important to continue to remind yourself, when looking at your perceived competitors, that they are on their own journey, and you are on yours too.

I know I know, I can hear you saying (or your Shitty Committee saying) '*but they are my competition, I am competing against them to land the job, the gig, the deal, the gold medal, the cup etc.*' and I hear you, I truly do. But when you see the likes of the athlete Elaine Thompson-Herah lining up to race the 100m final at the Olympics, or the swimmer Adam Peaty getting ready to dive into the pool for the 100m breaststroke, whilst they are aware of the competition lining up alongside them in the different lanes vying for a medal, they are completely focused on running or swimming their own race. If Peaty were to watch how his competitors were swimming in other lanes throughout the race, he wouldn't be focusing on his own lane, his technique and his ability to swim would be impacted, and his time and position in the race would be impacted too.

Instead, both Peaty and Thomspon-Herah, focus on themselves as their own competition, looking at their starts as they come out of the block, their techniques as they get into the race and the way they come to the finish line, all with the view of making small adjustments to improve and enhance their abilities as they go from race to race, season to season. This focus has led to Peaty breaking more than a dozen world records in the swimming pool, and Thompson-Herah, in 2021, becoming double Olympic champion over both 100m and 200m.

Let's take time to look at you and how you can slay in your lane. I want you to write down any area of your life that you want to succeed in. It could be anything from reaching your ideal weight all the way through to becoming the head of the company you currently work for. The focus here is to get specific and write down exactly what you want to slay in:

____

____

Now that you've written down the area you want to slay in, I want you to write down where you are at today in comparison to where you want to be to slay.

____

____

____

Good, you've completed the first two steps. For many, this part can be quite scary, as it could be that you are 2 stone (28lbs/12.7kg) from your ideal weight or 4 promotions away from landing your dream role. But bear with me, this is just The Shitty Committee kicking in, saying things like *'it's too far'*, *'it's going to take too long'*, *'it's out of reach' 'you're crazy to think you can achieve that'* – The Shitty Committee doesn't know when to stop.

But pay no attention to The Shitty Committee right now nor give it any fuel. We are focusing on how you can slay in your lane and so the next step I want you to take is to list all of your abilities or resources that you can tap into to slay. This could be the skills you've acquired, techniques you've learnt, or even the people who can support you on this journey to Slaydom, aka a more fulfilling life.

____

____

____

Let's go a step further. Are there any resources or abilities you need to slay in your lane that you currently don't have? This could be an individual like a personal trainer or a skill set like graphic design.

____

____

____

Good, you are making real progress here, getting clarity on where you want to slay, where you are at in comparison to being able to slay, what abilities you currently have, and what resources you need. I want you to remember this next quote:

Where your focus goes, your energy flows.

Remember Dick Fosbury earlier? He didn't focus his energy on the abilities he didn't have; he chose instead to focus on the resources he did have (his knowledge of mechanics) and his abilities (to jump over the bar backwards, head first) to allow him to slay in his lane. But this didn't come overnight. Fosbury put in the time and effort and continually worked on himself and his technique to get to a position where he ended up winning Gold at the Olympics, breaking the Olympic record in the process.

Applying this to yourself, your first task is to look at the resources and abilities you don't currently have, and be ruthless - ask yourself if you could benefit from upskilling and diversifying your skill set or is it something you could outsource. Allow me to share a quick insight from my own life. I always remember a quote that Tony Robbin's said at an event of his which I attended in 2017. He said, '*Hire your weaknesses.*' That was a real eye opener for me, as I was always the person that wanted to do everything to get me to where I am today. By doing so, it always slowed me down and held me back from slaying in my lane. So I made a conscious decision that rather than always being the one using my limited skill-set to do things I wasn't great at, such as design work, I would use designers from Fiverr.com to help me design the content I needed for my work. It would take them a tenth of the time that it would take me and, most of the time, it would be much better quality. This allowed me more time to focus on my strengths and enhancing them.

I can hear your Shitty Committee kicking in and saying, '*but Jack, I don't have the financial means to hire my weaknesses*' and I hear you when you say that, but this is tied to a belief you have inherited from someone or society that your Shitty Committee uses to keep you safe. Let me tell you, investing in yourself is the best investment you will ever make. If your finances don't allow you to invest in yourself, look at what budget you do have or offerings you could provide that could be used so that you can have others focus on your weaknesses whilst you focus on your strengths. As I mentioned before, I used fiverr.com to help me with a lot of my design work. When I was getting quotes from companies to design my self-care card deck, I couldn't afford the half of them, so I went to fiverr.com where the cost to design them was 15% of the prices being touted by design companies. The results were just as good, if not even better than what the design companies might have delivered.

If your finances mean that you currently have no income to hire your weaknesses, consider using your own skills to trade work quid-pro-quo. I have a great photographer friend named Jack Alexander and, when I needed to get PR shots for launching my business, I didn't have the kind of money that Jack rightly charges for his photography. As a compromise, we agreed that in return for his time spent in a photoshoot, I would deliver some coaching sessions. It's not just about the resources you have, but how resourceful you are, that will determine your ability to slay in your lane.

Take the time now to list the resources or abilities you don't have, working out which ones you can gain by working on or acquiring them yourself, and which ones you can outsource to others so that you can slay in your lane:

Resources or Abilities I Will Acquire

____

____

____

____

____

____

Resources or Abilities I Will Outsource

____

____

____

____

____

____

The next step to slaying in your lane is focusing on the pathway of where you are currently to where you want to be. For example, if you've never run a marathon before, it's extremely unlikely that you are going to be able to run one overnight. You need to build up your strength and stamina over a period of time, to get you to a point where you can run the 26.2 miles required. You will need a plan to complete a marathon, and that's exactly the same when slaying in your lane. For slaying in your lane is a marathon not a sprint. so I want you to make the time right now before moving on to the next chapter to focus on those incremental gains that you can make (no matter how small) to get you to where you need to go.

If your goal is to lose two stone in six months, you can start by breaking that goal down into smaller goals that seem less overwhelming, for every journey must start with a single step. Think about it: two stone over six months equates to 28lbs, which is roughly 4.7lbs per month or just over 1lb a week. I don't know about you but losing 1lb a week seems a lot less daunting to me than losing two stone that's for sure. From there you may want to then factor in what additional resources you need, be that a gym membership or a personal trainer. Once you have the appropriate resources, you can schedule those resources into your time to help you on your goal to slaying.

For whilst we know that eating less and exercising more will help us to lose weight, if it were that simple then why is it that in 2021 28% of UK adults are obese and over 36% are overweight? A lot of that is connected to our relationship with food and exercise. If you want to go a step deeper into slaying in your lane, it may not be enough to have a gym membership or purchase the right food; because if you are triggered by something or someone, The Shitty Committee is likely to kick in and, for many, food provides solace and comfort when we feel shit. As such, by being aware of your triggers and having an accountability partner, or additional support in a therapeutic capacity to help understand your relationship with food, it may also help you on your pathway to developing a healthier relationship with food which, over time, will help you move towards your goal of slaying that two stone.

What I want you to do is breakdown your pathway from where you are now to where you want to be, so that you can begin to slay in your lane. It can often help to reverse engineer this process. By reverse engineering the process, you envision having already succeeded in slaying in your lane where you are living a more fulfilling life, and you are retracing all the steps that you took in reverse to where you are currently at in order to slay. To do this, keep asking yourself the following questions as you map out your pathway to slay:

If reverse engineering:
What step did I take that got me to this next level?

If starting from where you're at:
What is the next step I need to take to get me closer to slaying?

Continue to ask yourself these questions until you map out your pathway to a more fulfilling life. If you head to the back of the book, under Index 1 (on pages 181 and 182), there are example frameworks of each version for you to fill out or use as a template to do in your own journal/diary. Then, why not make a physical copy that you can place somewhere you will see every day - on the wall, on the fridge, in your office, anywhere to remind you of the pathway you are on. If you feel like getting really creative, you could also use Gold stars to acknowledge each step once you've reached it.

Now that we've focused on how to slay in your lane, we are going to move to the next chapter where you will learn how to use inspiration to master The Shitty Committee to live a more fulfilling life.

12

IMITATE DON'T DUPLICATE

"If you're the smartest person in the room, you're in the wrong room." - Confucius

When I started to write this book, I felt like I was heading up shit creek without a paddle. I'd never written a book before and, whilst I have read hundreds if not thousands of books in my life, it doesn't mean I can write. As I finally got round to putting pen to paper, or should I say fingers to laptop, The Shitty Committee was saying '*What right do you have to write a book?*', '*No one cares what you have to say!*', '*You can't write for shit!*' These were limiting beliefs I had formed in my childhood, from my teachers who constantly picked up on and criticised my writing abilities all the way through to the bullies and family who would often silence me when I had something to say.

But despite what they had to say, and the limiting beliefs The Shitty Committee had formed to prevent me from writing this book, I knew I had something to share with others. Whilst the words I write, the stories I tell and the tools and techniques I share may not be for everyone, if they even help one person to live a more fulfilling life and prevent them from taking their life like my brother did, that, for me, would be worth it. With that as my fuel to drive me forward into taking action, I still needed to know how to put a book together that would connect with readers, flow naturally and have people coming away from reading it more informed and more able to live a fulfilling life – and this is where modelling comes in.

When I talk about modelling, I don't mean becoming Naomi Campbell and strutting your stuff down the runway - though her confidence as she walks is something we could all learn from. I mean modelling in terms of the behaviours, approaches, and the mindset of other people who you regard as successful. I have never had any desire to be a singer, but I respect and admire the work ethic of artists like Mariah Carey and Ed Sheeran that have gone on to have continued global success in their respective careers. For it is one thing to gain success, but it is a whole different thing to maintain it. Success does, however, leave clues along the way, and no matter in which area you are looking to live a more fulfilling life, the habits, routines, techniques and tools of those who are successful can help to guide you on the pathway to a more fulfilling life. Furthermore, those individuals who you choose to model, can also teach you how to avoid some of the mistakes they made on the way to becoming successful, so that you can stand on the shoulders of these giants.

It was the illustrious poet and civil rights activist, Maya Angelou, who once infamously said:

'Do the best you can until you know better, then when you know better, do better.'

I love this quote but, as you will know by now, I often find that quotes from others don't always paint the full picture and I would like to build on Ms Angelou's words to say:

Do the best you can until you know better, for once you know better you can do better, and then and only then can you BE better.

Or if I was to break it down into a simpler model, it would be:

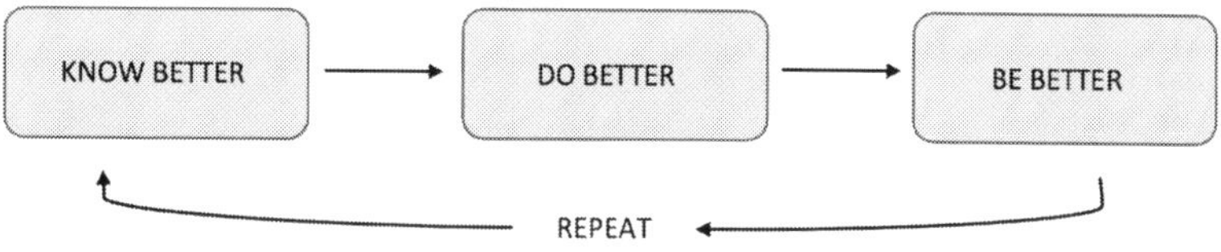

Figure 3 - Know Better, Do Better, Be Better Model

By modelling someone else on something we want to achieve in life, we gain the knowledge to know how to approach things, so that we can then move forward and do better. As a result, we can be better than we were before we acquired that knowledge. If we continue to see this as a continuous loop and repeat the cycle, continuing to gain and acquire knowledge along the pathway to a more fulfilling life, we can make those changes, no matter how big or small to help drive us forward.

So how do we go about modelling others? One of the leading writers on the area of modelling is a gentleman by the name of Tim Ferris. Ferris shot to fame following the release of his book, '*The Four-Hour Work Week*', where he detailed a load of different techniques that helped him on his way from earning $40,000 per year and working 80-hours a week, to earning $40,000 per month and working 4-hours a week. Strategies including how to eliminate 50% of your work in 48 hours using the principles he had learnt from a forgotten Italian economist, to how you can outsource your life, using a whole host of resources, to free up your time to focus on what truly matters, Ferris's book became the go to book for anyone who wanted to work smarter, not harder.

Following on from the success of his book, Ferris went on to release a whole host of other books, including one of my favourite books I've ever read called, '*Tool Of Titans*'. In the book, Ferris interviewed over 100 individuals who are leaders in the fields of Health, Wealth or Wisdom and shared the tactics, routines and habits they use to make them the leaders they are today. If you haven't had a chance to check out either book, I suggest you add them to your reading lists; if you've already read them, read them again, for each time you read the books you are at a different stage in your life and new pearls of wisdom will speak to you in ways they couldn't before.

Modelling is all about helping you to level up, to stand on the shoulders of giants, to help you to become the best version of yourself. Over the next few pages, I am going to list my top five modelling tips that I use in my everyday life that will also help you to master The Shitty Committee and live a more fulfilling life.

1. STACKING

I know that no matter what I do, The Shitty Committee is always going to be there ready to pounce at a moment's notice, whether it's when I am feeling run down, exhausted, or I've hit an obstacle. And so, what I do each and every day is stack my morning with a regular routine that is going to motivate me and move me into the right space to take on the day ahead and overcome any obstacles that life may throw my way.

Stacking is the process in putting together a number of activities, one following on from another, that will keep your momentum going. Everyone will have a different approach to this but, for me, my mornings look like this:

6:00am - Wake Up
6:10am - Go for a 5-mile run
7:00am - Jump into an ice-cold shower
7:10am - Meditate
7:30am - Grab my iced coffee and breakfast
7:45am - Review my schedule for the day
8:00am - Hit my day with the wind in my sails

If you look at many of the world's leading people in any field, they tend to wake up before or as the sun is rising, knowing that the early bird catches the worm. For it is always important to seize the day on the pathway to a more fulfilling life. The more hours you have in the day to do that, the better the chances are of you moving in the right direction.

Exercising first thing in the morning not only gets your body moving and the blood pumping around your body, but it helps to release the dopamine and serotonin chemicals that are responsible for our happiness and well-being. A little-known fact is that emotions - if you break the word down - is energy in motion. By using the morning to carry out a form of exercise, it pushes you in the right direction and, also, as I like to say:

To Inspire We Must Perspire

A cold shower after a long run helps not only to wake up the body even more, but to help the muscles to recuperate. Whenever I'm in Los Angeles, the first thing I do when I land is head to Upgrade Labs, to use their Cryo chamber, as two minutes in the chamber at -180C is like a shot of energy that helps me get over my jetlag and prepare me to hit the ground running. This allows me to be as productive as I can with my time in the city of dreams.

After that I tap into the app, Insight Timer, which is my go-to meditation app to help me to clear my mind of any thoughts The Shitty Committee is trying to throw my way and focus on the present moment, whether that be with the guidance of one of the guided meditations or using ambient sound and repeating a mantra to take on the day ahead.

By that point I am ready to fuel up and, for me, that means it's time to hit the caffeine and grab a morning snack. I usually like to do this with no distractions, so that I can truly savour the taste of the iced coffee and snack that I am eating, rather than doing it whilst looking at my phone or working on my laptop. If I'm lucky and the weather is nice enough I'll eat outside in the garden. Finally, before I get stuck into the day, I take the time to review what I have planned, making any key notes before I kickstart what I need to get done.

This morning ritual that I have put in place every weekday morning and most weekends really helps me to not only build my energy but to also know that, before I start my work for the day, I have already achieved something by taking care of both my body and my mind. It leaves me in the best state to start my day, giving myself something to celebrate. When I speak to those individuals whom I want to model to become a better version of myself, they all have similar morning routines and, although there may be variations in the start time, the length of time devoted, or the activities they include in their morning routine, all of them make sure to take care of both their body and their mind before starting the day.

What routine can you create for yourself that takes care of both your body and your mind to start your day the right way and keep The Shitty Committee at bay? The clearer and more specific you can get when doing this, the better – think about the time you start your routine and the length of time you need for each activity as well as how frequently you will do your routine (daily vs weekdays). As I often say, '*Don't delay what you can do today*', so draw up that routine and start putting it into practice in the next 24 hours.

MY MORNING ROUTINE

_______ AM | __________________________

_______ AM | __________________________

_______ AM | __________________________

_______ AM | __________________________

_______ AM | __________________________

One thing to remember when planning your morning routine is that it takes roughly 30 days to form a habit. You need to persevere with your routine so that it becomes embedded in your body and mind to become second nature. There are going to be mornings that you don't want to get up or days when the weather isn't so great outside that you don't want to do it, but it is on those days, more than any other, that you need to dig deep and push through, for you will feel so much better on the other side.

2. PREPARATION

As I mentioned above there are going to be days when you are tired, when the elements are working against you, or when you come up against an obstacle on the way to a more fulfilling life, and this is where preparation comes in key to help you master The Shitty Committee.

Remember this – ***If you fail to prepare, then be prepared to fail***. Successful people always prepare ahead of time, or get someone to do the preparation for them, as we all want to follow the path of least resistance. And so the more time we take to prepare, the easier it will be when we need to face whatever we need to do to live a more fulfilling life.

If you are going for a run every morning, make sure your running gear is laid out for you the night before so that The Shitty Committee doesn't have the ability to say to you, '*it's too much effort to get ready, let's stay in bed.*' Trying to hit your ideal weight? Spend time once or twice a week preparing your food, including snacks, so that it is easier to grab and go on those days where you have less energy. We all know that it is on those days that The Shitty Committee says it will be easier to just order a takeaway and you can go back to your healthy eating tomorrow (that is a slippery slope to hell if it becomes a habit in itself, unless it's worked in as one of your cheat days).

If you are working on a business, a project or a goal, make the time to draw up a schedule of ***what*** you need to do, ***when*** you need to do it and ***how*** you are going to do it. Identify the resources that you need in order to move forward and make sure they are easily accessible to you when working, so that The Shitty Committee can't use the excuse that you don't have access to it and therefore it can wait until tomorrow. Tomorrow isn't promised to anyone so, as I said before, don't delay what you can do today.

What things can you do to prepare for a more fulfilling life, how are you going to incorporate that into your routine so that The Shitty Committee doesn't get all up in your business and try and take you away from living a more fulfilling life?

3. PROTECTING YOUR TIME

We all have 24 hours in a day and 168 hours in a week and though we all have different commitments and responsibilities, the excuse that you don't have enough time doesn't mean shit when someone who has the exact same situation as you is flourishing. That excuse is The Shitty Committee trying to stop you from leaving the familiar and is saying thing to you like, '*but x means that I can't do y*' or '*until I have x I can't do y*' thereby keeping you stuck. Remember this:

If you don't sacrifice for what you want, then what you want becomes the sacrifice.

The Shitty Committee tries to be sneaky and says '*if/when I have x then I will be able to do y*', but the '*if/when…then*' line is keeping you stuck! I know I've used this excuse many times myself in the past. If I had or when I have more money, if I had or when I have more time, if I had or when I have more resources…then I will be able to live a more fulfilling life, start writing a book, build my own business etc. But I came to learn by looking at and modelling others that the people who are the most successful in life focus less on the resources they want or need and more on being resourceful with the resources they have, including their time.

Time is one of the most valuable resources any of us have and it is one thing we can never get back once it's gone. To live a more fulfilling life, it's not about working more hours than ever before, but being smarter with the hours you do work, so that you are able to propel yourself forward. Over the years I have learned a few techniques from various people, that have helped me to protect my time so that I can focus on fulfilling my full potential.

The first and foremost when it comes to business is to window your email times. Remember *your inbox is someone else's to do list.* By windowing the times you check your emails to maybe two or three one hour periods a day, you no longer become chained to your inbox, becoming its slave caught up in email chains or emails that take you away from what truly matters. If you are away on holiday but need to check your emails because of time sensitive opportunities, why not use this template out-of-office reply that I've created below.

"Thank you for your email. I am currently out of the office but will checking my emails twice a day at ____ and ____ for 30 minutes. If your email is urgent, please resend your email with the words URGENT in the subject title, and I will get back to you in one of these windows. All other emails will be replied to when I return from my break on __ /__ /__."

By doing this, you are communicating your boundaries, making it clear you will only respond to urgent matters and then, when you do go to check your emails at those windows, you can filter your inbox to bring up the urgent emails only. This avoids getting caught up in any other emails, therefore protecting your time and getting straight to the important stuff. Of course, there are going to be some douchebags that are going to resend their email with the word 'Urgent' in the subject when the content of the email isn't urgent at all, but that is on them, not you. A classic real-world example of this was when I was working with an artist who insisted on having Fiji water ahead of his TV performance (which was still 6-hours away). At the same time, I was dealing with the fact that the TV show didn't want the artist to perform their new song but the hit from the year before; and another artist I was working with had to cancel a whole host of promo due to falling ill. But no, artist number one kept bugging me for their Fiji water. To them, not having their room temperature Fiji water was a category five problem in their world but, to me, it wasn't even a tropical storm. I had bigger problems to deal with. Someone is always going to think that their issue is more urgent than whatever urgent is for you at that moment in time. So be clear with your boundaries and, if need be, delegate to someone else like I did in the case of the Fiji incident.

Also, when it comes to protecting your time, make sure you remove any distractions that can prevent you from staying in a flow state (that state you find yourself in when you are inspired, motivated and focused on what you are doing) and gives The Shitty Committee an opening to take you down a rabbit hole, away from what you need to be doing to live a more fulfilling life. A human gets distracted, on average, every 42 seconds, as we attach our minds to one of the thousands of thoughts or external stimulants that come across our mind. With your digital devices, turn off any and all notifications that may distract you from focusing on what needs to get done. For me, that means closing down Outlook on my laptop whilst I write this book so that email notifications do not come in. It also means closing down all the tabs on my browser, bar one, in case I need to cross reference something that I am writing. With my mobile, I turn my phone onto Airplane Mode during the periods I have assigned to writing, for there is no emergency for me that can't wait a couple of hours (unless a family member is critically ill).

If turning your phone onto Airplane Mode isn't an option, then go into your settings and turn off all the notifications on your apps. For those notifications are little dopamine hits, designed to make you feel good/important and having you reach for your phone. If you have an Apple device, each week you get an update on the time spent on each device and that will show you how long you spend in each app. Take the time to review this update to see how much time you are devoting to something that isn't helping you to live a more fulfilling life. Consider how you can utilise that time instead by diverting it into working on yourself, your project etc. If need be, put a time limit on those apps to enforce those boundaries.

If you occupy a busy space, invest in some noise cancellation headphones to drown out any noise distractions that will take you away from what you need to focus on. If you are responsible for others, i.e. children, wake up an hour before them to focus on what you need to get done or work out a schedule that between a certain time period you are not to be disturbed. Utilise family members, babysitters or, if the children are old enough, closing the door of the space you are in and reaffirming you are not to be disturbed with a note on the door.

These are just a few ideas of what you can do to protect your time so that you can focus on what needs to get done and stay in a hyper-focused state. This way, The Shitty Committee will have fewer opportunities to veer you off track. What are you going to do to protect your time and how are you going to do it?

4. HIRE YOUR WEAKNESSES

I know I've mentioned this before but it's worth repeating again. If you aren't good at something, hire someone else to do it for you so that you can focus on your strengths. This applies both in your everyday life as well as whatever it is you are specifically working on to live a more fulfilling life.

If cleaning isn't your thing and you hate doing it, then why not hire someone else to do your cleaning for you. Many may see it as an unnecessary expense and The Shitty Committee will say '*why are you wasting your money when you could be doing this yourself?*', but you aren't ***many*** people; you want to model those successful people who are living a more fulfilling life, and many of them will hire someone to help them. They aren't wasting their money as The Shitty Committee wants you to believe, they are investing their money wisely. For time is the most valuable currency of all and you can't buy time back once it's gone. Those 4 hours spent cleaning, could have been four hours spent towards creating a more fulfilling life, and aren't you worth investing your time in that and outsourcing the cleaning?

Thinking of what you need to do to live a more fulfilling life. Make a list of thc strengths you have and the weaknesses you need to hire to make your more fulfilling life a reality. Look at the list of your weaknesses and, if they are not an essential requirement that you need to develop yourself to live a more fulfilling life, hire someone else to take care of it for you. Not good at organising? Hire a virtual PA. Not good at design work? Hire a designer on Fiverr.-com. Not good at sticking to a routine in the gym? Hire a personal trainer. Whatever you deem as a weakness, use the support available around you to help you. If money is an obstacle, get resourceful - approach students at college or university to help you out or offer to swap services, their skills in exchange for yours, to help propel you forward.

Write down the weaknesses you see that can prevent you from moving forward on the pathway to a more fulfilling life. Then identify the people or resources you can tap into to take care of those weaknesses. Whilst you are at it, why not put this book down now and take action to delegate those weaknesses, so you can focus on your strengths to keep the momentum moving forward.

5. WHAT WOULD X DO?

Last but not least, in terms of modelling, think '*What would X Do?*' If you are modelling the success of others before you, you aren't necessarily going to have access to them. You may have access to their books, podcasts, and interviews but not them as individuals; and the material you do have access to may not give you the specific answers you need to help you model what they would do. As such, one important question that you should always equip yourself with, is '*What Would ___________ Do?*'

Oprah is the person I most often look to model in my life and, I have created a card that specifically asks me that question. I keep it with me or place it in front of me when needing guidance and inspiration, for any time that I hit a wall or The Shitty Committee starts to worm its way into my consciousness.

So, who is the person you want to model? Have you identified them? If not, take the time now to identify who you would like to model and create a visual cue card to keep with you that reminds you of that question whenever you need it.

Figure 4 - Example of the card I created, that you can replicate yourself with the person you choose to model.

BONUS TIP

One of my first bosses in the music industry, Hugh Goldsmith, who has gone on to become a mentor and dear friend of mine once gave me some great advice. He said, '*Jack, always aim to be the least knowledgeable person in the room.*' Ever since he gave me that advice, I have followed it. If you are in a room where you are the least knowledgeable on a topic in question, you have an opportunity to grow and flourish. If you become the most knowledgeable/skilled person in the room, then you have outgrown your environment and it's time to level up. ***For you can't be what you can't see***. Let's look at tennis as an example. If you are a tennis player and you were playing tennis regularly against someone less experienced than you, would you continue to grow as a player or would you stay at the same level you are at? Now compare that to if you were to playing regularly against Novak Djokovic or Serena Williams, would you grow as a tennis player then? As you continue on the pathway to a more fulfilling life, continuously check if you are the most knowledgeable/skilled person in the room. If you are, you will plateau and not grow; you will not level up and those who aren't growing are the ones who are being left behind. So don't get left behind, keep moving forward and find that room where you can continue to grow.

Modelling the behaviours, values and beliefs of others that inspire you, who have paved the pathway to a fulfilling life, can help you get to your destination. But what happens when you hit an obstacle or setback on that pathway to live a more fulfilling life? In the next chapter 'Don't Call It A Comeback', we are going to look in more detail at how to look for the rainbow in every storm and comeback even stronger than before.

13

DON'T CALL IT A COMEBACK

"Your attitude determines your altitude." – Zig Ziglar

In May 2005, Rafa Benitez had led Liverpool FC to the Champions League final in Istanbul, one of football's most coveted trophies, to take on an AC Milan side who were heavy favourites to claim the cup for a seventh time. Liverpool themselves were no strangers to the silverware having already won the title four times since the Champions League was formed 50 years prior (when it was then known as the European Cup). Yet on that night in Istanbul, Carlo Ancelotti's team sheet of players read like a who's who of serial winners, including the Brazilian World Cup winning captain Cafu and the legendary Paolo Maldini who had already won the Champions League final with AC Milan four times.

From the outset, it appeared that it was going to require something special for Liverpool to win the final and, as the ball was placed on the centre point in the Atatürk Olympic Stadium, within a minute of the kick-off it all started to go horribly wrong for Liverpool; AC Milan's Maldini volleyed the ball into the net from an

Andrea Pirlo free-kick. As the match wore on, it was clear that AC Milan were the better team and, with the first half drawing to a close, in the final 6 minutes Hernan Crespo managed to net two more goals past the Liverpool goalkeeper, Dudek, for AC Milan to enter half-time with a 3-0 lead over Liverpool.

The pundits had written Liverpool off in the half-time commentary, many fans in the stadium looked defeated and heartbroken and, even as I watched the match with my friend Anthony in a pub in South-East London, having been a fan of Liverpool since I can remember, I had conceded defeat for my beloved team even though there was still the second half to go. What Liverpool needed was a miracle.

Now only a select number of people know what was said in that Liverpool dressing room at half-time but, as both teams re-emerged to the field in the second half, something had shifted in the Liverpool players. In six of the most magical minutes in football history, Liverpool rendered AC Milan powerless, as Steven Gerard headed the ball past Dida to make it 3-1, before Vladimir Smicir sliced the ball into the bottom corner to make it 3-2. The belief of the Liverpool supporters in the crowd, the pundits and all those watching on TV, all knew now that Liverpool were back in contention. Mere moments later, Alonso stepped up to take a penalty after Gerrard had been fouled and, although the penalty was saved, Alonso came in double-lively with the rebound to launch the ball in the back of the net and even the score at 3-3.

Liverpool held on to the 3-3 score until full time and, as extra time came in to play, there was a real feeling that Liverpool could win the match. After extra time, the game was still tied at 3-3 and so the match was taken to penalties.

Both Liverpool and AC Milan had won their last European cups on penalty shoot-outs, but one team wouldn't be so lucky this time. Milan were chosen to go first and Serginho shot the ball over the crossbar, with Dudek mimicking Bruce Grobbelaar's infamous spaghetti legs antics during the 1984 penalty shoot-out against Roma to distract the player. Liverpool were next and scored their first two penalties by Hamann and Cisse, whilst Perlo from AC

Milan missed, giving Liverpool a 2-0 advantage. Tomassan and Kaka netted the ball for AC Milan bringing the score back to 2-2, making for a captivating but tense environment both for the players on the pitch and all watching on. With Smicer stepping up to the penalty spot next and scoring to make it 3-2 for Liverpool, and with still another shot for Liverpool left to take, it was all on Shevchenko's shoulders to keep AC Milan in the game. Shevchenko shot the ball straight down the middle and as, Dudek went to the right, he managed to block the shot with his left hand to give Liverpool the victory, winning by 3-2 on penalties.

People all around the world were calling it one of the greatest sporting comebacks of all time, with Argentine legend Diego Maradona saying '*Even the Brazil team that won the 1970 World Cup could not have staged a comeback with Milan leading 3-0.*' Liverpool returned from Istanbul the next day as European champions, with over 1 million people flooding the streets to welcome the team home to celebrate, arguably, one of the greatest football matches there has ever been.

There are so many great lessons that can be taken from this match, including don't count yourself out of what you want to achieve in life just because things aren't going your way, or there is no such thing as plain sailing on your way to a more fulfilling life. For as you set sail on your journey to live a more fulfilling life, you are going to come across some choppy waters. There will be storms that you face which may lead your boat to capsize or winds that you come up against that alter your path. This resistance may leave you feeling defeated, like you can't go on any longer, and that the pathway to a more fulfilling life is not worth weathering the storm. But in life, not all storms come to disrupt, some come to clear the path.

As mentioned in the chapter, Weathering The Storm, there are three types of people who ride a boat through a storm:

1. **The Optimist** – who expects the wind to change
2. **The Pessimist** – who complains about the wind
3. **The Realist** – who adjusts the sails

In the case of Liverpool, at half-time they were down but they weren't out and so rather than being pessimistic about the situation, they had to be realists. They had to change their tactics and their approach to the second half. Under the leadership of Benitez, the team took the data they had acquired from the first half and made a series of tactical changes, from player formation on the pitch to substitutions. They adapted their playing strategy to strengthen their chances of being more competitive in the game and, as you saw, those changes worked, leading Liverpool on to victory.

On the way to a more fulfilling life, as you hit those choppy waters, or that storm, The Shitty Committee is going to turn up in full force, trying to convince you to turn back to the harbour where it's safe, rather than sail forward to the promised land. It perceives danger all around you and wants to keep you safe, but being safe doesn't equal fulfilling. As theologist William G. T. Shedd once said, '*A ship is safe in the harbour, but that's not what it's built for.*' Ask AC Milan - they were comfortable with their 3-0 lead, which led to them playing it safe in the second half and, in those six minutes of magic, they threw away their lead and were caught on the backfoot; and though they attempted to, they never fully recovered.

If you want something badly enough, you will fight tooth and nail for it. Just ask Anna-Mae, aka Ms Tina Turner.

Tina Turner was born Anna-Mae Bullock on 26th November 1939 in Brownsville Tennessee. At the tender age of 17, Turner began her singing career with Ike Turner's Kings Of Rhythm as one of the featured vocalists of the group. She appeared under the name Little Ann on her first record, Boxtop, in 1958 and two years later in 1960 with the song '*A Fool In Love*', which picked up traction with local DJs. During this period Ike Turner decided to change her name to Tina and added his surname Turner, whilst also trademarking the name as a form of protection, so that should Tina leave like previous singers of Kings Of Rhythm had, he could replace her with another 'Tina Turner'.

Over the next 16 years, Ike and Tina Turner went on to have mainstream success with a number of hits including '*Proud Mary*', '*River Deep Mountain High*', '*Nutbush City Limits*' and countless others all over the world. But as their success continued to grow and the spotlight shone more and more on Tina, Ike's temper also grew as did his addiction to cocaine. Ike's controlling and abusive ways with Tina were constant and unrelenting until one day, on 1st July 1976 where upon arriving in Dallas from LA for a gig that evening, Ike and Tina got into a physical alteration en-route to the hotel.

Shortly after arriving at the hotel, Tina fled Ike for good, seeking refuge at a friend's house; and three weeks later filed for divorce. The divorce would go on for nearly two years before being finalised at the end of March 1978. During their time together, Ike had not only retained control of all of the finances in their marriage but in their working relationship too, which left Tina without a penny to her name and a rising number of debts. Tina was willing to concede everything in the divorce, but she refused to concede the rights to her stage name. After almost two years, Ike finally relented and gave Anna-Mae her stage name, Tina Turner, bringing their lengthy divorce to a close.

During that period and into the early 1980s, Tina's star had continued to fall, leading many to consider her a nostalgia act who had already had her time in the spotlight. She picked up whatever gigs she could to make ends meet, both to provide for her children and the mountain of debts that needed to be paid. But whilst Tina Turner was down, she was not out, for the fire inside of her burned brighter than the fire outside that had tried to bring her down, from Ike to the debts, to the naysayers.

Though she had still been releasing music during that period, it hadn't been connecting; but all of that was to change in 1983 when Turner signed with Capitol Records. In November that year, she released a cover of Al Green's '*Let's Stay Together*' and, surprised by the track's success, Capitol green-lit a studio album. Just seven months later in May 1984, Turner released the album '*Private Dancer*' which would shoot her into the stratosphere with a string of Top 10 hits, including global No.1 hit '*What's Love Got To Do With It?*' that would also go on to win the Grammy for Record of the Year. As the rest of the 1980s progressed, Turner would go on to release a string of hit songs, ending the decade with her signature anthem '*The Best*'.

The 90s saw Turner's star continue to shine brightly, with a biopic of her life '*What's Love Got To Do With It?*' released to cinemas in 1993. It landed the cast best actor and actress nominations at the Oscars and secured Turner the opportunity to record the theme song to the Bond film, '*Golden Eye*', in 1995. She closed out the millennium with her tenth and final solo album, '*Twenty Four Seven*', with the her tour the following year becoming the highest grossing tour worldwide, bringing in over $120 million.

You see, once again, like Liverpool at half-time in the Champions League final, many had written Turner off following her divorce. But she never wrote herself off or allow her experiences to give fuel to The Shitty Committee; she never gave up during the dark times and continued to persevere, which resulted in Turner shining even brighter than she had during her time with Ike.

As you continue to embark on living a more fulfilling life and take massive action towards that goal, know that, like Liverpool or Tina Turner, there will be obstacles that you will come up against. It could be a team, an individual or, more likely than not, The Shitty Committee. What these two examples show is that success will come eventually to those who continue to push forward through adversity.

So anytime you come up against a challenge that has set you back on your pathway to a more fulfilling life, I want you to say **'Here comes AFGO.'** Now what does AFGO stand for I hear you ask? AFGO stands for:

Another **F**ucking **G**rowth **O**pportunity

Remember, life doesn't happen *to* you, it happens ***for*** you. Any obstacle, challenge, or setback that comes across your pathway is an opportunity for you to grow. Think of them as growing pains, if you will. Though it may be painful at the time to go through, you will grow from it and stand taller, see further, and have more clarity on the pathway to a more fulfilling life.

When you are experiencing an AFGO, I want you to ask yourself the following three questions:

1. What went well in this situation?
2. What did I learn?
3. What can I do differently moving forward?

When you go back to the Champions League final match, Benitez was asking these exact same questions of himself and his team during half time to help them grow in the second half and win the match. He reviewed what went well in the first half for Liverpool, he learnt the tactics and techniques of AC Milan that were leading them to win at half-time, and he adjusted his approach to the match in the second half to lead them to victory.

You see, I don't believe in the word failure, I see it only as feedback. If we take the time to learn from what happens, we can grow from it. But if you do believe in failure, then fail forward, don't let that perceived failure knock you back. Beyonce lost out to another singer on the TV talent show, '*Star Search*', in 1993; Walt Disney was told that a mouse would never work; J.K. Rowling's first book in the *Harry Potter* series was rejected 12 times by publishers; and Oprah Winfrey was told she was unfit for TV. Now imagine if any of these people had let those setbacks stop them from pursuing their dreams and fulfilling their full potential.

There are a million stories similar to those examples above of setbacks, rejections, losses and failures where the individuals concerned didn't give up on their dreams; they lived to tell the tale today. And **YOU** <u>will</u> be one of them too. You will come across that person who rejects your idea, who tells you you're not the right fit, who won't offer you the funding to bring your idea to life, but don't let that give fuel to The Shitty Committee; use it as a 'Here comes AFGO' moment and ask yourself those three questions to help you learn and grow from the situation and become even stronger than you were before.

Think of a challenge you have come up against recently that has given fuel to The Shitty Committee to keep you stuck or make you turn away from where you want to head and write it down below:

____

____

____

Now you have done that, answer the three Here Comes AFGO questions below:

1. What went well in that situation?

____

____

____

2. What did I learn?

____

____

____

3. What can I do differently moving forward?

____

____

____

I'm not naïve enough to think it's as easy as just thinking 'Here comes AFGO' and asking yourself those three questions to get you back on track; but as you continue to practice Here comes AFGO, your comeback or bounce back rate (the time it takes you to recover from something) will improve with every obstacle you face as you move upwards on the steps to change.

The steps to change (known more commonly as the transtheoretical model developed by Carlo DiClementi and James Prochaska) help to show where you are at on the pathway to a more fulfilling life and how far you may be knocked back when hitting an obstacle on that pathway.

Figure 5 - Transtheoretical Model (Steps To Change)

Depending on the blow that an obstacle causes you, it may have knocked you down from step six '*I can do it*' to step two, '*I can't do it*'. You may even find yourself there for a week before you are able to dust yourself off, pick yourself up, and start working your way back up the steps to change. The next time you face an obstacle, you may be that little bit stronger from thinking through the mindset of Here Comes AFGO. As such that obstacle may only have you falling back one step rather than four or it may only take a day to bounce back rather than a week. Then the next time, that knock back may only take you half a day, the next an hour and then before you know it, it will be only a matter of minutes before you are able to bounce back from any obstacle on your pathway to that more fulfilling life.

Every journey is different; for some, it may be two steps forward one step back, whilst for others it may be a giant leap to step seven, *'I will do it'*. As Here Comes AFGO helps to highlight, even a setback can help you to see the bigger picture, gain more clarity, and, if you are stuck on a certain step for a period of time, it may be that you are taking in the view to explore what options and resources you may need. There are often many different pathways to a more fulfilling life, but they all lead to the same destination. Taking that time can help you become clearer on the steps you need to make that more fulfilling life a reality.

It also helps to remind yourself that the lower down the steps to change you are, the more likely it is that The Shitty Committee will show up and hold you back from that more fulfilling life. This is why it is so important to keep tapping into 'Here Comes AFGO' any time you hit an obstacle. It will help you to shift from a fixed mindset and being a slave to The Shitty Committee to a growth mindset, where you move up those stairs on the pathway to a more fulfilling life. As Henry Ford once famously said,

'Whether you think you can or you can't, you're right.'

If you think you can't do it and stay in that mindset on that step to change, then you're right, you can't; but if you are willing to put one foot in front of the other and take it step by step and if you believe you can do it, that driving force will help to propel you forward even further to *'I will do it'*, and then *'I did it'*.

Take a look back at those steps to change and think to yourself, where am I on the pathway to a more fulfilling life right now? Once you have identified that, I want you to think again about 'Here

Comes AFGO' and use this approach to help you move up the stairway to that more fulfilling life at the very top.

The journey to appreciate the view from the top of that staircase can be hard work and so, before we take a look at that view in the final chapter, we need to ensure we are fuelled up and ready to conquer those steps. In the next chapter, 'Where Are My M&M's?' we will explore this further by getting you ready to step into your spotlight.

14

WHERE ARE MY M&M'S?

"Today is a great day to manifest the shit out of some abundance."
– A Sassy Queen
"Motivation is what gets you started, habit is what keeps you going."
– Jim Ryun
"A good mentor teaches you how to think, not what to think."
- Proverb

It's 8:30pm at the O2 Arena in London, it's the first of three sold-out London shows, and the venue is packed. The support act has just come off stage and the anticipation is building for the headline act Fiona, who has finally brought her tour to London after months on the road playing to fans in cities all around the world. Her family and friends are in the audience, as are the team members who have been with her since the start. Her record label, publisher, booking agency, and promoter are all there too, to celebrate this milestone in her career, her first sold-out arena show in her hometown. The electricity in the audience is palpable and, as showtime nears, Mexican waves go around the arena as people sing along to her hits. This is a big moment for Fiona and her fans but, backstage, it is a whole different story.

Sitting in her dressing room, Fiona is having a full-blown panic attack. Her Shitty Committee has kicked into high gear, causing her to feel anxious about the upcoming show, and she starts to catastrophise. The Shitty Committee is telling her '*You're going to fuck up in front of everyone and be the laughing stock of London*', '*You're going to forget all the words to your songs and people are gonna walk out and leave.*' The negative thoughts, that were endless, continued to make her feel worse and worse. She even started planning her escape from The O2 Arena so she could avoid performing, anything to make sure that what The Shitty Committee was saying didn't come true. And that's when the panic attack hit.

This wasn't the first time a panic attack had happened to Fiona, but it was by far the worst to date. Her management had brought me in, in anticipation that this may occur. My job was to help Fiona work through her panic attacks and master The Shitty Committee, even if just for that night, so that she would be able to go ahead with the show. Over the next half an hour, I worked with her to reclaim control from The Shitty Committee and how it was making her feel, using techniques that I will outline over the subsequent pages, to help her go out and perform.

Nowadays, there are so many artists that speak openly about their battles with performance anxiety when they have shows and concerts, from Zayn Malik, formerly of One Direction, to Adele, as well as numerous entertainers and sporting professionals. There are so many people who, in everyday settings, also get social or performance anxiety in crowds or when speaking in meetings or conferences. It has therefore become one of the most common issues that people want help in overcoming in the course of my work, to help them live a more fulfilling life.

Every time I deliver a workshop, webinar, or a keynote speech at a conference I, too, get performance anxiety. There have been countless times in my formative years that I have missed out on opportunities, turning them down because The Shitty Committee keeps telling me that I'm going to fuck up, make a tit out of myself, become a laughing stock, never be welcomed back again, or get fired from my job. And so, I'd rather not risk that chance of humiliation, no matter how small, than to have it confirmed. Pretty ruthless, right? You see, The Shitty Committee likes to stay in its comfort zone of things it knows and, if it perceives anything as a threat, like speaking or performing in front of an audience, going into a room full of strangers, or doing something you've never done before, it is going to do and say whatever it can to keep you in your comfort zone.

However, we are only born with two fears: the fear of falling and the fear of loud noises. The rest of our fears are learned along the way as The Shitty Committee gains strength and takes on the values and beliefs that you are being exposed to. Anytime The Shitty Committee perceives a fear, it kickstarts your adrenal glands to start producing adrenaline, as it feels a threat is imminent. If we can harness that adrenaline, we can turn it into excitement and use that energy to face the fear. If, on the other hand, The Shitty Committee harnesses it, it turns it into anxiety and triggers our fight, flight, freeze or flock response to help keep us safe and within our comfort zone.

For any of you that haven't heard of the fight, flight, freeze or flock response, when The Shitty Committee perceives a threat (real or imagined), it can be broken down as follows:

Fight – our fight response is used to fight off whatever imminent threat The Shitty Committee perceives
Flight – our flight response is used to escape the threat as soon as possible
Freeze – our freeze response is used to shut down our systems to conserve energy and/or go unnoticed
Flock – our flock response is used to seek safety in numbers as soon as possible

The fight, flight, freeze and flock response is a great asset to have when faced with a real life danger, like being confronted by a Tiger. But with the case of Fiona, her performance anxiety, though feeling very real, was a perceived fear that gave fuel to The Shitty Committee. Whilst we can't get rid of the perceived threats that The Shitty Committee wants to protect us from, we can equip ourselves with tools and techniques that can keep us in the driving seat to help us fulfil our full potential and not be hindered by The Shitty Committee's power.

To do this, I like to use a model taught to me by Renee Jain and Dr Shefali Tsarbury; which I have expanded upon to incorporate additional layers, called the 'Where Are My M&M's?' model (which I tell every performer I work with to include on their rider). You might be wondering what on earth chocolate M&M's have to do with keeping The Shitty Committee at bay and is that why I hear artists demanding only a certain colour of M&M on their tour rider? To answer the first question, no, it's not the chocolate M&M's that I'm asking you to have to help you stop feeling like shit and live a more fulfilling life, but a bunch of six M's (like the six different colours you find in M&M's) to help overcome performance anxiety.

In answer to the second question, when you hear about artists and their riders outlining that they only want a certain colour M&M or something very specific, 9 times out of 10, it has nothing to do with the item in question but more to ensure that the venue or promoter is paying attention to the rider. If the touring crew arrive and they don't, for example, see blue M&M's in the dressing room, they know that the rider hasn't been fully read, which could mean that a key production requirement needed for health and safety may also have been missed. It immediately alerts the tour, production or stage manager to a potential issue, giving them time to ensure all the necessary requirements to carry out the show are in place.

The six Ms that form the Where Are My M&M's? model are:

1. Movement
2. Motivation

3. Mindfulness
4. Mirage
5. Mentorship
6. Metabolism

Over the next few pages, I will break down each of these Ms in more detail.

1. MOVEMENT

The first M is Movement.

When your adrenal glands kick in and start producing adrenaline, that adrenaline has to go somewhere. It's a form of energy that, if harnessed correctly, can be used to create excitement and get you ready for what you are about to face. Think about when you see players before a football match or athletes sprinting out of the blocks before the race starts. For them, this movement isn't only about warming up those muscles that they are about to utilise, but about harnessing that adrenaline which is starting to pump around the body rather than letting The Shitty Committee turn it into anxiety.

Another thing you'll often see is people changing their physiology in the position they are standing or sitting. For example, imagine you walk into a bar and you see two people. The first is slouched over the table drinking their beer, shoulders dropped, head hanging low, like their whole body is closing in on itself. The second, is sitting tall, head high, shoulders back with a smile on their face. Who of the two looks more appealing to you, if you had to choose one to go and talk to? The second one, right?

You see, changing our physical state, in terms of movement, no matter how big or small, can help to change our mindset. Whether it's doing cardio exercises like running on the treadmill and yoga or moving our bodies in slightly different ways to open up our physiology more, it helps to trigger our dopamine and serotonin (the feel-good and well-being chemicals) in our brain. Even striking a power pose like a superhero or pounding your chest creates movement to help harness the adrenaline that's pumping around your body and turning it into excitement.

When you think about the movements you could incorporate into your life that help ahead of something that may cause you anxiety and prevent you from stepping into the spotlight, what movements could you have in your M&M's jar to pull from?

Physical Exercise

____

Posture

____

Power Move

____

2. MOTIVATION

The second M is Motivation.

If you're like me, it takes me a while to get motivated to do certain things, including writing this book you are reading (the motivation to start writing this book has taken more than two years – that's how strong The Shitty Committee was until I got going). Despite what many of my friends, family and former students think, I am extremely lazy when it comes to doing things - and I own that. However, whilst I might be extremely lazy, I become hyper-focused when I set my mind to accomplishing something and I motivate myself in a number of different ways to prevent The Shitty Committee from showing up and sabotaging my ability to achieve my goals.

When you see boxer Anthony Joshua, MMA fighter Conor McGregor or even The Rock in his WWE days prepare for a fight or make their way to the ring, they motivate themselves by playing songs to get them pumped up and into the mindset to take on their opponent. Similarly, when you are in the gym or running on the street, you have a soundtrack playing that keeps you motivated to keep pushing through that extra rep, that longer run, that faster row or that additional mile on the bike, to go beyond your mind's limits to not only achieve your full potential, but often to surpass it.

Alongside songs that motivate you, another way you can motivate yourself is through affirmations and mantras. Most people question the difference between an affirmation and a mantra and, in the simplest of terms, affirmations are motivational and usually said out loud, whereas mantras are more sacred, often accompanying meditation and repeated within.

Examples of affirmations used by public figures include:

Actress/Singer J-Lo – '*You are youthful and timeless at every age.*'
TV Mogul Shonda Rhimes – '*You have a right to the universe. You are given that right simply by being born.*'
Tennis champion Serena Williams – '*No one can tell you who you are except for you.*'

Examples of popular mantras include:

'*I create my own path and walk it with joy.*'
'*My positive thoughts guide me to new heights.*'
'*I am not afraid to be wrong.*'

In addition to these, I have a couple of additional ideas to get you started in thinking about your own mantras or affirmations if you have never had one before. Give it some thought and fill in the blank below:

I AM ____________________

TODAY I GIVE MY INNER GOD / GODDESS (DELETE AS APPROPRIATE) PERMISSION TO ________________

You can use those two examples as your motivational affirmations or mantras and you can build on them. In addition, you can use an image, speech, podcast or book that motivates you to help you achieve your full potential. What are your motivation options that will go into your M&M's jar?

Go to song to get you motivated

____

Go to playlist to keep you motivated

____

Go to mantra to get you motivated

____

Go to affirmation to get you motivated

____

Go to image to get you motivated

____

Go to speech/podcast to get you motivated

____

Go to book to get you motivated

____

3. MINDFULNESS

The third M is Mindfulness.

Mindfulness has become one of those buzz words that has been kicked around a lot in recent times by the media and companies. It is intended to help people's mental health and well-being and, whilst it often gets a bad rap, it is one of the most important M's in the Where Are My M&M's? model to quieten The Shitty Committee, keep you grounded, and help you to focus on the present.

Imagine a hurricane. A hurricane is a powerful force of nature that comes along and, dependent on its strength (category), can destroy everything in its path. However, in the hurricane is the eye of the storm, the centre that is almost peaceful and quiet, with the winds swirling around it. The Shitty Committee is like a hurricane in situations where there is a perceived threat and, if you allow The Shitty Committee to take hold, it will sweep you up and make you spiral out of control. The purpose of mindfulness is to ground you in the eye of the storm, so that you stay present and unaffected by what may be going on around you, both outside and within your head.

To do this, most people often turn to one of three things:

1. Meditation
2. Breathing
3. Savouring

Meditation helps to focus our attention inwards and to become an observer of our thoughts instead of attached to them, like laying in a cloud watching the clouds float by in the sky. Though stemming from India several thousand years ago, it is practised all over the world today and there are several apps that can help you to mediate in a variety of different styles. These include ambient music meditation, guided meditation and transcendental mediation.

By focusing on our breath, we are able to help our body slow down our heartbeat which is helping to pump the adrenaline produced by our adrenal glands around our body. Focusing on our breath also triggers our parasympathetic nervous system, which is responsible for helping our body to rest, digest and relax, bringing us back to a state of calm and being present.

Savouring is a technique where you take the time to really savour something, usually the food which you are eating, taking in its taste, texture and enjoying it fully. It is often recommended to use a raisin for this, but I often use chocolate.

Mindfulness isn't restricted to these three areas. If you watched the Tokyo Olympics, you will have likely seen Tom Daley (Diver) sitting poolside between dives knitting away. This helped Tom to keep his mind focused and grounded and not allow The Shitty Committee to consume his thoughts with what could go wrong in the competition, or worrying about his competitors. As a result, Tom finally secured the Olympic Gold that had eluded him in the previous three Olympic games.

When looking at your own Mindfulness options, below are some examples you can explore:

Meditation apps you can use include:
Insight Timer, Headspace, Calm

Breathing techniques include:
Breathe in for four, hold for four, breath out for four

Savouring can include:
Eating chocolate, watching the sunset

Activities that promote mindfulness include:
Knitting, Origami, Gardening

Take the time to try out different meditation apps, breathing techniques, savouring options and mindfulness activities to find which one(s) work for you, and then utilise them when needed to help you step into the spotlight.

4. MIRAGE

The fourth M is Mirage.

I've slightly cheated with this M as I wanted to use the word 'visualisation' to help you overcome The Shitty Committee, but mirage works just as well. Have you ever woken up from a dream and it seems to be so real until you fully wake up, or put on a 3D headset and enter a different world which seems completely believable to the eye. That's because our brain can't tell the difference between what is perceived and what is real.

By creating a mirage or visualising the outcome you want to achieve, you can trick the mind into thinking a different outcome to what The Shitty Committee might be filling your mind with. You often hear top athletes talk about visualising their races ahead of a competition, going through each and every step, embedding into their mind what will happen and how they will attack their performance to get them ready to fulfil their potential.

Creating a mirage of your future too, can help your mind become focused on what you want to achieve. By painting as full a picture as possible in your mind of what you want to achieve down to the smallest of details, and continually tapping into that image, it can act as an alternative image in your mind to the horror film that The Shitty Committee might be trying to play. This can also be done in physical form, by creating a vision board of all the things you envision you'll have in a more fulfilling life (a dream house, a blank cheque with your ideal salary on, performing to a sold-out arena)

. . .

The mirage can also tie into the mindfulness, where you can create a place in your mind that brings you calmness, joy, motivation, happiness or any other positive emotion or feeling, to feed your inner goddess or superhero.

What would your internal mirage (visualisation) look like to help you achieve your full potential?

____

____

What will you put on your vision board, that symbolises you living a more fulfilling life?

____

____

____

____

Where is that one place you can visualise, that brings you joy, motivation, happiness or any other positive emotion you need to tap into, to help you quieten The Shitty Committee and step into your spotlight?

____

____

5.MENTORSHIP

The fifth M is Mentorship.

One of the core human needs we all have is the need to belong and, whilst Abraham Maslow put belonging as the third level on his hierarchy of needs, I believe that a sense of belonging is the foundation of any human need, before physiological or safety needs.

When you are on the pathway to fulfilling your potential, there are going to be obstacles along the way. And any obstacle that comes in your way is an opportunity for The Shitty Committee to show up to stop you from continuing to move towards a more fulfilling life. The great unknown can be a scary place, especially the path less travelled, yet it isn't a journey you have to take alone. For as the expression goes, a problem shared is a problem halved.

As mentioned in Chapter 12, as you embark or continue on your pathway to a more fulfilling life, there will be people who have walked a similar path to you before and will have gained various insights along the way. These are the people who will be able to help you to not make the same mistakes as they did and to stay on track.

When thinking of what you are currently looking to achieve, can you identify mentors that could help you to fulfil your potential? They can be those you know and have relationships with, or those who you don't know.

Mentors that I could tap into include:

____

____

____

Now you have identified your mentors, I want you to make a plan of how you can tap into their knowledge to help you on your pathway to a more fulfilling life. If you know them, do you need to schedule a meeting? Do you need frequent accountability calls to keep you on track? If you are unable to access them directly, what material of theirs is at your disposal, that you can consume and learn from them? Courses, books, interviews, podcasts?

____

____

____

____

____

Mentors can also be expanded to include coaches, trainers and therapists, to help you on the pathway to a more fulfilling life. If you feel alongside the mentor/s you've identified above you could do with some additional support, then why not reach out for professional support through agencies such as BACP for therapists or ICF for coaches.

6. METABOLISM

The sixth and final M is Metabolism.

As we mentioned back in Chapter 4, what you consume can determine how you feel about yourself, and give fuel to The Shitty Committee to make you feel like shit, preventing you from starting to live a more fulfilling life. Three things you need to be mindful of consuming in environments or situations that you feel anxious in and may provide an opportunity for The Shitty Committee to prey on your anxieties include, caffeine, alcohol and junk food. I appreciate that might be easier said than done, for I do love me a red bull and my diet is definitely more junk food than healthy (though I'm working on that) and until New Years Day 2018 I used to be a binge drinker when it came to alcohol. But by being aware that these three things can enhance your anxiety and reducing or removing them in anxiety-provoking situations, it gives less fuel to The Shitty Committee to run away with.

Metabolism isn't only about what food and drink we consume, but also the other things we consume that can make us feel like shit including social media and the news. Then, when we face ourselves in an anxiety-provoking situation, because we feel like shit we are in a weaker state to fight off The Shitty Committee and find ourselves fighting an uphill battle.

Think about what you consume in terms of food, drink, social media, entertainment and even your friends and write down a list of anything that may make you feel like shit and stops you from stepping into the spotlight. How can you cut down those things you consume or cut it out completely?

The Where Are My M&M's? model is the perfect tool for you to utilise to prevent The Shitty Committee from showing up in situations where you need to step into your spotlight, on your pathway to a more fulfilling life. Like the actual M&M's, different people will have different ones they prefer (the orange flavoured ones) or avoid (the nut ones), and so whilst there are six different M's here to choose from, it may be that some of the M's work better for you than others, whilst some may not work for you at all - that's okay. However, it is my recommendation that you find at least two or three that work for you (though preferably all six) and then stack them (refer back to Chapter 12, if you need a reminder on what stacking is). This will allow you to carry out one M directly after the other, to strengthen your inner resilience so that it can take on any obstacle The Shitty Committee tries to throw your way.

Throughout this book, you will have discovered or been reminded of a variety of different tools and techniques you can use, to stop The Shitty Committee making you feel like shit and to help you start living a more fulfilling life. I have every confidence that if you implement these tools and techniques, you will immediately start living a more fulfilling life. I look forward to hearing your stories about how you overcame The Shitty Committee and what that has allowed you to do with your life. But before we bring this book to a close there is one final chapter I want to end with and that's the view from the top once you are living a more fulfilling life.

CONCLUSION

15

THE VIEW FROM THE TOP

"The people who are crazy enough to think they can change the world often do."
– Walter Isaacson

Have you heard of the story about the businessman and the fisherman? One morning, a businessman was visiting a beach in Brazil when he came across a fisherman coming towards the shore in a small boat, having caught several big fish. The businessman, intrigued by the fisherman catching so many fish so early in the morning, enquired '*How long does it take you to catch so many fish?*' '*Oh just a short while*' the fisherman responded.

Impressed by his abilities to catch so many fish in such a short while, the businessman asked, '*Then why don't you stay out at sea longer and catch even more?*' to which the fisherman replied '*This is enough to feed my whole family.*' The businessman, perplexed by this then asked, '*So what do you do for the rest of the day?*' and the fisherman replied '*Well, I wake up before sunrise to go out to sea and catch a few fish. I then come back and play with my kids. In the afternoon, I take a nap with my wife and then, in the evening, I join my friends in the village for a drink, we play guitar, sing and dance into the night.'*

The businessman then offered up a suggestion to the fisherman. *'I have a PhD in business management and I could help you to become a more successful person. From now on, you should spend more time at sea and try to catch as many fish as possible. When you have saved enough money, you could buy a bigger boat and catch even more fish. Soon you will be able to afford to buy more boats, set up your own company, your own production plant for canned food, and a distribution network. By then, you will have moved out of this village and to Sao Paulo, where you can set up HQ to manage your other branches."*

Once the businessman had finished sharing his vision, the fisherman asked, *'And then what?'* to which the businessman responded, *'After that you can live like a king in your own house and, when the time is right, you can float your business on the stock exchange, and you will be rich.'* Pressing further, the fisherman asked *'And after that?'* The businessman then continued *"After that you can finally retire, you can move to a house by the fishing village, wake up early in the morning, catch a few fish, then return home to play with the kids, have a nap in the afternoon with your wife and then when the evening comes you can join your friends for a drink, play the guitar and sing and dance into the night!'*

The fisherman was puzzled, *'Isn't that what I am doing now?'*

Everyone's vision of how to live a more fulfilling life is going to be different as both the businessman and the fisherman show in the story just shared. Some may want to continue growing, expanding and evolving the pathway to a more fulfilling life, whilst some people may be content exactly where they are when they reach that destination they envisioned for a more fulfilling life. There is no right or wrong option here, but when you get to the top of the mountain having achieved a more fulfilling life, it is important to reflect on these three key things:

1. Remembering your why
2. Maintain the habits that led you to a more fulfilling life, or creating new ones to sustain it

3. Seeking support

1. REMEMBERING YOUR WHY

Remembering your why is like the Northern Star in the midnight sky that helps to light and guide the way, keeping you on track and focused on living a more fulfilling life. Back in Chapter 8 when we looked at The Pain In The (Secondary) Gain, by doing the 7 Levels Deep exercise, you will have uncovered why in your life you remained stuck and how The Shitty Committee was holding you back from living a more fulfilling life; you learnt how to turn that into the fuel to propel you forward. For some, it's that they want to be in control whilst, for others, they want to be around to watch their children grow up. Whatever your reason for wanting to live a more fulfilling life, it is important to continue to remember your why so that you don't become complacent.

I remember when I lived in LA, I was fortunate enough to live in a house with floor to ceiling windows in the Hollywood Hills at the top of Runyan Canyon. When I first moved in, I would open my curtains every morning to take in the sunrise and show appreciation for the day as I looked over Hollywood and Los Angeles beneath me. Yet as time wore on, I became complacent and would keep the curtains closed in the morning because my room faced eastwards getting the early morning sun, ignoring the privileged position I was in to have a room with a view. I eventually ended up having to say goodbye to that view as I moved back to London, where the view out of my bedroom window was nowhere near as beautiful.

You see, once we get what we want in life, that job, that car, that ideal weight, that house, that partner and so on, we can become complacent and not take time to appreciate it. And so, by constantly remembering your why, it can keep you in a place of gratitude for all that you have when living a more fulfilling life. Those that continue to live a fulfilling life constantly remind themselves of their why, whether their why is printed on the wall of their company, tattooed on their body, or saved as their screensaver; they ensure they have a constant reminder of their why to help them to continue living a more fulfilling life.

To further help keep you in a place of gratitude, practising what I call the attitude of gratitude daily will help ensure you keep The Shitty Committee at bay. By focusing on the positive in your life, you will begin attracting more of it, rather than allowing The Shitty Committee to get you to focus purely on the negative. Whether you practise the attitude of gratitude each morning as you start your day, in a team meeting at work, around the dinner table with family or friends, or in a journal at the end of the day, focusing on what you are grateful for, no matter how big or small, can help you to continue being appreciative of living a more fulfilling life.

Why not take the time now to write down three things you are grateful for:

1. ______________________________
2. ______________________________
3. ______________________________

And whilst you are at it, why not take the time to remind yourself why you want to live a more fulfilling life in the area you are looking at and how you plan to continue reminding yourself of your why:

____

____

____

2. MAINTAINING THE HABITS THAT LED YOU TO A MORE FULFILLING LIFE OR CREATING NEW ONES TO SUSTAIN IT

Following that pathway to the top of the mountain to live a more fulfilling life is hard, but maintaining it is even harder. This is where so many individuals end up falling backwards down the hill as The Shitty Committee creeps back in. It tells you to take the foot of the pedal, questions everything you are doing and, slowly but surely, chips away at you, until you find yourself back where you started or potentially even further away from living a more fulfilling life than when you embarked on that journey.

It's so important to take in the view from the top, when you have reached the goal of living a more fulfilling life. Savour that moment and reward yourself for all the hard work and effort you have put in to living a more fulfilling life, for that is a massive achievement and should not be overlooked. However, if you see achieving a more fulfilling life as the end goal, rather than maintaining and sustaining it, you are giving permission to The Shitty Committee to come in and take away that fulfilling life from you.

Over the years when I worked in the music industry, and even now in my practice as a coach and therapist, I find so many artists whose goal it is to land a major record deal because they believe that is the key to getting the chart success that they have dreamed off. However, I like to remind them that once they sign a major record deal, that is when the real work only truly begins. Roughly 95% of artists that sign to a major record label never go on to have commercial success in the charts. I remember working with one girl-group at Sony in the mid-2000s, where even though almost half a million pounds was spent on them, their music was never released commercially, in large part due to the girls not working hard enough or wanting it badly enough. And this is a story that has been repeated time and again at record labels.

This is true in other areas too. If leading a more fulfilling life is having your own business rather than working for someone else's business, you may go on to set up your own company, work extremely hard and make a profit or even breakeven in the first year. Nowadays, most businesses may not breakeven or start making a profit until much further down the line; just look at the likes of Spotify, Amazon and countless others who took years to start turning a profit and relied on funding rounds to keep the business moving forward. A study conducted by The Telegraph showed that over 60% of companies go out of business in the first three years; in some cases, it may be out of the owner's control but, in most, it is a lack of commitment to the business, an unwillingness to adjust the sails to pivot to a more profitable and sustainable business model, and a lack of resourcefulness to meet the needs of running a business. If living a more fulfilling life is reaching an ideal weight, and by going on a diet and exercising more it helps the person get there, you will often find that person will revert to old habits and behaviour once they have achieved their ideal weight. They may cut back on the frequency of exercise or bring back food and drinks that have been cut out when they reach their ideal weight. This is why studies show that 95% of diets fail.

The key to continuing to live a more fulfilling life is to continually put into practice the habits that lead or led you to a more fulfilling life and make them part of your everyday lifestyle. Whether it be some of the tools and techniques I have shared in this book that you can turn into habits or the habits you have identified of people who inspire you, by turning them into habits you practise daily, you will be much more likely to sustain a more fulfilling life. As the expression goes:

If you are persistent, you will get it. If you are consistent, you will keep it.

You may also require a different set of habits to maintain a more fulfilling life than the habits that you used to gain it. As such, identifying those habits are going to be key to helping you. This leads us into the third and final area which will help to ensure you continue to enjoy the view from the top of living a more fulfilling life.

3. SEEKING SUPPORT

I think we can all agree that Albert Einstein was an extremely insightful man, responsible for many a great discovery and inventions over his life, but one quote of his stands out for me over all other things he achieved in his life:

No problem can be solved from the same level of consciousness that created it.

As discussed in Chapter 9, Weathering The Storm, there are going to be problems that come up in our lives no matter which station we are at. Whether it's along the pathway to a more fulfilling life, at the very beginning, or even when we are living it, problems are going to occur and the mindset that created the problem isn't going to be the same mindset that will get us out of it.

Often that mindset is just The Shitty Committee showing up to cause us issues, but it can also often be the case that problems turn up when you are living a more fulfilling life. As in recent times, it could be a pandemic, a recession, or a bereavement that can lead to that more fulfilling life slipping through your fingers. This highlights the need to have the right support around you to ensure you can weather any storm that comes across your path.

So what support do you require to ensure you are able to maintain a more fulfilling life? Remember, if it is a skill set requirement, then hire your weaknesses to support you through any problems that may arise, be that a crisis management team to handle a PR issue for your business, a financial advisor to ensure you are investing your money wisely or a team to delegate work down to now that you have the resources to do so, allowing you to focus more on your why and allowing the team to focus on the what, when, where and how.

It is also important to remember that the pathway to a more fulfilling life is emptier for those who walk that extra mile to achieve it and, often, it can be lonely once you reach the top. Whilst that solitude can be quite transcendent, it also gives ample opportunities for The Shitty Committee to show up, questioning whether you will be able to sustain a more fulfilling life now you have gained it, as many executives in business experience, which is why so many have executive coaching. If you want to focus on continuing to master The Shitty Committee, then why not hire a professional coach, therapist, NLP practitioner or a Transitionist like myself to help you navigate whatever is coming up for you? That could be working on yesterday for a better today or working on today for a better tomorrow, giving you the time and space to expand your perspective and thinking, and identify and work on your blind spots, allowing yourself to become the best version you can be.

As this book comes to a close, I want you to remember that you have the power within you to master The Shitty Committee and that you deserve to live a more fulfilling life. I truly believe that. I hope the various stories that have been shared, the tools and techniques highlighted, and the questions asked, have helped to ignite the fire inside of you so that you can implement what you have learnt across these pages to gain the momentum you need to move along that pathway to a more fulfilling life. For now, you know better and, knowing you can do better will enable you to be better.

ACKNOWLEDGEMENTS

There are quite a few people I would like to thank for helping on this pathway towards fulfilling my dream of becoming a published author.

Lynne Best; my editor, for helping me to become a better writer, improving my grammar, challenging me to enhance the messages within these pages and just for being an inspirational woman. **Betina Bendtsen Vangsfeldt** for embarking on this journey alongside me and being my accountability partner – everything changes but you. **Leah Stockford** for all your invaluable advice, words of wisdom and for helping me bring my vision for The Shitty Committee to life. **Mandy Plumb**, for being my marketing guru and brainstorming partner in crime. **Katie Greenway**, my PR princess who helped me to understand and navigate the publishing world. **Olly Brooks** for being the best assistant I could have ever asked for. **Adrianna Irvine** for helping me with my own Shitty Committee. **Jin Jin** for being there on the worst day of my life, **Ryan Walter** for being there at the start of my new chapter and being the first to believe in me.

Also a massive thank you goes out to all of those who have helped me throughout the creation of this book. From the questions I had on the designs, to the titles and wording as I brought the book together, including Lou Lebentz, Thando Zulu, Joe Lever, Laura Henderson (my bean flicker), Nirvana Chelvachandan (Lady in Red), Phil Loutsis (my fellow black-belt in origami), David Palmstrom, Sarita Tamber, Daniel Scott, Celine Bonner and James Butterfield (The Kentish K**ts), Maria, Jason Allen (XOXO GG), Ryan Keen, Fee, Sharon Eden, Sean Johnson, Sam Williams, Stef Faleo, Caitlin Geehan (my Sony P.I.C), Bonnie Kemplay, Jevan Levy, Cat McCabe (aka my Cat Flap), Anthony Hurd (my life-long friend), Lindsay Doherty (aka Yasdnil), Marwa El-Atribi (my side-eye sister), Omar El-Atribi (thank you for getting my physiology and psychology aligned), Trina Smith, Aimee Dean. Betty, Gemma, Laurence Boakes, Kelly Thatcher, Geoff Langston, Rosie Krneta, Cézanne Tobin, Kelly Betts (my pocket rocket princess) Kelly Whitehead (my fairy-godsister and Hampstead wanderer), Ellie Moore, Jonathan Robinson, Jack Alexander (for making me look half decent), Rose Warn (my fellow rambler), June Allen (my pathway pioneer), Liana Bullard (for always keeping it real), Lewis Shaw and Adam Davies (for bringing my digital space to life).

To all my therapists over the years, thank you for helping me work through my issues. To all my clients who have and continue to entrust me in helping them with their own Shitty Committee, thank you for putting your trust in me. And to anyone who has previously been part of my External Shitty Committee that has made me feel like shit and stopped me living a more fulfilling life, I thank you for the lessons you taught me.

INDEX 1

CREATING YOUR PATHWAY TOWARDS YOUR MORE FULFILLING LIFE.

If you want to visualise your journey towards living a more fulfilling life, then why not try out the below exercise to help map out your pathway towards a more fulfilling life.

Question 1 - Where am I currently at in relation to living a more fulfilling life on a scale of 1 to 10?

____

Question 2 - What step/s do I need to take to move from ___ (insert number from previous question) to ____ (the next number up) ?

____

____

____

____

Question 3 - What would be the next step/s I need to take to get me from ____ (the step you moved to in question 2) to ___ (the next step up) ?

____

____

____

____

Repeat question 3 until you get to 9 out of 10 on your scale.

(Continued on the next page)

Final Question - What are the last step/s I need to take to enable me to enable me to live a more fulfilling life?

____
____
____
____

RETRACING YOUR PATHWAY TOWARDS A MORE FULFILLING LIFE.

If you prefer to, you can visualise having already achieved a more fulfilling life and retrace your steps, working out what you needed along the way to get to that more fulfilling life.

Question 1 - What is your more fulfilling life?

____

Question 2 - What was the final step you took to achieve a more fulfilling life?

____
____
____
____

Question 3 - What was the step I took before that to help me step towards a more fulfilling life?

____
____
____
____

Repeat question 3 until you get to where you are today in comparison to the more fulfilling life you envision for yourself.

INDEX 2

If you ran out of space in a certain section of the book, or need additional space to write down your thoughts, please use the below to bring your thoughts to life.

INDEX 3

ABOUT THE AUTHOR

Jack Williamson is a powerhouse in both the coaching and therapy worlds. A former award-winning music industry executive, he is an international speaker, podcaster, best-selling author and works with many leading entertainment and sporting professionals.

Through Jack's philanthropic work with both Music & You and his Point One Project foundation, he continues to improve and sustain the mental health and well-being of over 200,000 music industry professionals and is on track to increase that number to two million by the end of the decade.

If you found this book helpful and feel others could benefit from this book, leaving a review by scanning the QR code on the left, can help my mission in ensuring that no one else loses the battle to their Shitty Committee, like my brother did.

To find out more; including working with Jack, sign up to Jack's newsletter, by heading to www.jackwilliamson.co.uk. You can also follow him on Instagram and Linked In @JackChristopherWilliamson.

Printed in Great Britain
by Amazon

67845833R00116